A GIFT FOR:

....

FROM:

....

DATE:

....

COUNTRY SOUL

INSPIRING STORIES *of* HEARTACHE
turned into HOPE

Cara Whitney

FOREWORD BY DAN WHITNEY,
"LARRY THE CABLE GUY"

Thomas Nelson®
Since 1798

Published in Nashville, Tennessee, by Thomas Nelson. Thomas Nelson is a registered trademark of HarperCollins Christian Publishing, Inc.

Names and identifying characteristics of some individuals have been changed to preserve their privacy.

Published in association with the literary agency of WordServe Literary Group, Ltd., www.wordserveliterary.com.

Photographs on pages 4, 6, 11, 19, 22, 27, 32, 44, 48, 56–57, 65, 74, 82, 90, 98, 135, 142, 146, 152, 154, 160, 169, 175, 176, and 200 are by Erik Johnson, erikjohnsonphotography.com.

Photo on page 71 is by Joel Sartore.

The remaining photos are used under license from Shutterstock.com.

Thomas Nelson titles may be purchased in bulk for educational, business, fundraising, or sales promotional use. For information, please email SpecialMarkets@ThomasNelson.com.

Any internet addresses, phone numbers, or company or product information printed in this book are offered as a resource and are not intended in any way to be or to imply an endorsement by Thomas Nelson, nor does Thomas Nelson vouch for the existence, content, or services of these sites, phone numbers, companies, or products beyond the life of this book.

Cover design by Jennifer Greenwalt
Interior design by Kristy Edwards

ISBN 978-1-4002-3381-6 (audiobook)
ISBN 978-1-4002-3380-9 (eBook)
ISBN 978-1-4002-3378-6 (HC)

Printed in India

22 23 24 25 26 REP 10 9 8 7 6 5 4 3 2 1

CONTENTS

PART 1: GOD'S SPIRIT MAKES US LOVING AND HAPPY

PART 2: GOD'S SPIRIT MAKES US
PEACEFUL AND PATIENT

PART 3: GOD'S SPIRIT MAKES US KIND AND GOOD

PART 4: GOD'S SPIRIT MAKES US FAITHFUL

PART 5: GOD'S SPIRIT MAKES US GENTLE

PART 6: GOD'S SPIRIT MAKES US SELF-CONTROLLED

FOREWORD

Farm-Strong Faith: A Note from Dan Whitney (aka "Larry the Cable Guy")

This is my wife's fourth book. She's become the Stephen King of Christian book writing, minus the violent, satanic overtones. But I digress. She has been called to bring light into a dark, fallen world, and watching the Holy Spirit work through her is so awesome. I mean, someone who literally had no idea she had this spiritual gift of communicating through writing is showing people the love Jesus has for us. It's a blessing to watch her drop whatever she's doing at a certain moment and say, "God just gave me a thought," and then run into her office and pound out a chapter two hours later. The Lord definitely works in mysterious ways.

All of us who have come to accept Jesus in our hearts and the hope He gives us have a personal testimony, and this book contains many testimonies. They range from stories of folks whose lives went down a dark road to others who were raised as Christians but fell away. You don't need an elaborate testimony. All you need is the final sentence in your life: that you have come to know Jesus, and He has set you free. That is what changes a life. I love reading testimonials of how people from all different walks of life came to answer the door knock of Christ. It strengthens my faith listening to the joy that others have attained and seeing their lives totally transformed through Jesus Christ. The great I Am. The way and the absolute truth.

Nothing makes me tear up with happiness more than reading testimonies of how Jesus completely turned around the lives of the hurting, set them free, and filled them with hope. It's such an amazing tool to reach others who need that hope. Different people in all different circumstances in life, sharing their life of redemption with others. It just makes me smile so much. God is so good.

What's your testimony? Remember: it doesn't have to be elaborate. Nor does it have to be Stephen King dark to be effective. It just needs the last sentence: that Jesus lives in your heart and has set you free. That's the main part. Enjoy this book; it's life changing.

Dan Whitney—Larry the Cable Guy, Cara's husband, and underwear model

INTRODUCTION

Clean Slate: Old Shoes, New Soles

Up until a few years ago, the saying "walk a mile in someone else's shoes" was just something that adults would say to me so I might recognize that someone else has a life more difficult than my own. I'm pretty sure we are all aware of the situations people can fall into or be born into. There is always someone who has it worse than we do.

Sin made life hard for all of us.

One day, while helping my friend load the back of his SUV with some luggage, my eye caught sight of a pair of old, worn-out cowboy boots scrunched and ragged in the corner of his trunk. Suddenly, that annoying saying about other people's footwear took on a whole new meaning. *It takes a lot of stamina, commitment, and discipline to scar and bend a pair of leather boots like that*, I thought. Knowing personally that my friend has had to walk through some tough situations in life, I realized that his battered boots reflect his perseverance through all of it.

Our quality of life isn't based on the worldview that it's all "the luck of the draw." The quality of our lives is based on our confident expectation that the marathon we are all running leads to something better up ahead.

My friend's race was set before him by God. In other words, his boots are already taken. We have our own. Instead of studying what it must be like to set our feet in someone else's situation, I'd rather study how he was able to wake up every morning and keep going through some of the hardest miles of his life. His testimony is living proof that we are all going to be okay if we keep our eyes focused on Jesus, who is ready to take us into His arms at the end of this race.

Jesus blazed the first trail, and He showed us how He did it despite the fact that His human life was full of struggles He did not deserve.

We deserve our consequences. Yet sometimes God chooses to give our bad decisions a pass. Other times, due to no fault of our own, the manure spreader just lets loose all over us. How we push through it and then share with others the ways the Lord has worked in our lives is a great reminder to other believers that there are rewards for staying in the race and never giving up, even when we screw up.

Our Father is perfecting us, day by day, so that we can better serve Him.

Our Christian testimony doesn't end with our conversion experience. In fact, once you make that commitment to follow Jesus, that's when things get really interesting as you'll see in the stories that follow.

PART 1

God's Spirit Makes Us Loving and Happy

1

TRIPPING OVER SELF-DOUBT

"As the Father has loved me, so have I loved you. Now
remain in my love. If you keep my commands, you will
remain in my love, just as I have kept my Father's commands
and remain in his love. I have told you this so that my
joy may be in you and that your joy may be complete."
JOHN 15:9–11

I'm convinced that my pony Cupcake has come to our Nebraska farm for one reason: to provide companionship to Tucker, my stout Shetland. While Cupcake adores him, she doesn't care too much for people. That includes me.

For the first few years, Cupcake and I didn't have much of a relationship. Instead, we shared what I'd describe as an "understanding." We'd both go about our business—me tending to the endless chores on the farm and her swooning over Tucker. We kept our interactions simple, and believe me: I was content with it. Why complicate an arrangement that appeared to be going so well? And for doing such a great job of basically worshiping the ground Tucker walked on, I would pay Cupcake in food, shelter, and excellent vet care.

But as each day passed, and as our connections grew more and more robotic, I couldn't help wondering why. *What would it take to get this horse to warm up to me?* I'd ask myself. *Why does she have so much distrust for humans?*

I would bet the farm that some sort of past trauma blocks her from growing close to people—especially from trusting them. Every creature has a story, and Cupcake is no exception.

Whenever I needed to halter her, Cupcake would tense up with fear as the rope went over her head. She seemed to stand in obedience, perfectly still—almost as if she were trying to make herself invisible. I got the feeling Cupcake expected to be beaten down if she didn't comply. So, if I absolutely didn't have to interact with her—like to catch her for the farrier or something—I'd reluctantly choose to leave her alone. It seemed Cupcake was happiest when she was ignored.

Psychologists tell us that when humans feel stressed or frightened, they may launch into a fight-or-flight response. Sometimes they freeze so as to appear invisible.

Was Cupcake doing this? Regardless, something had to change.

It bothered me that this beautiful creature was living in such distress. I needed to soothe and comfort Cupcake, gradually giving her extra attention. I decided to let her out to graze in the yard, and then I'd walk up to her and hand her a treat—never expecting anything in return or asking anything more of her. And after about six months of doing this trust dance—one step forward, two steps back—Cupcake started coming around. I'd step back, giving my girl some space, and then I'd move two steps forward, spending a little extra time with her. Eventually, I was able to touch her face without a halter and without her sweet little body seizing up with distrust.

Finally, I could be trusted! Well, sort of.

Even after all this hard work and months of consistent loving care,

WISDOM
FROM THE
HORSE FARM

The Holy Spirit fills us with
God's perfect agape love.

I had gained only a little trust. Cupcake was still relapsing into her old, timid ways—tensing up, making it clear that she didn't want human interaction.

Why did she still doubt me, even after all I had done for her? I'd brush my pony and ask her that question: "Cupcake, don't you know me by now? Can't you see how much I love you? Why can't you let go of the past and begin trusting me?"

While I didn't grow up in a Christian home, it wasn't a bad beginning. In fact, my life was pretty good, and I was well provided for. I had loving parents and a supportive family. I never went hungry; I had a warm, comfy bed; and I was taught self-reliance.

Yet in spite of all these advantages, I grew into adulthood making some extremely poor choices, or as I like to call them, my own "self-inflicted traumas." Striving to live as a self-reliant woman meant responding to all those mistakes with the same pat answers: *Figure it out*, I'd tell myself, right along with, *Hey, you're on your own, girl!*

The world calls this *tough love*, and for so many years, I responded to life's bumps and challenges with my standard fight-or-flight response. In a sense, I'd make myself invisible.

By the time I reached my twenties, I believed I had possibly been created by mistake or maybe even created for something bad. Since "good" people were created for heaven, this bad egg was excluded. I was on my own.

So, picture my puzzlement as I watched Christ's love played out on the big screen in the blockbuster movie *The Passion of the Christ*. I was blown away when Jesus petitioned on behalf of His executioners, "Father, forgive them, for they do not know what they are doing" (Luke 23:34). *Wow!* I thought. *Now, those folks are some bad eggs, yet Jesus is also willing to forgive them. I need to know more about this Jesus.*

Fast-forward a decade. After extensive study of the resurrection of Jesus Christ, I found enough evidence to believe it as fact. Jesus did rise from the dead. Our sins were paid in full by Him at the cross. I made the choice to believe it, but it still took another two years to break up with my self-reliance and give Jesus the life that, in reality, I was never in control of. Eventually, I gave Him my whole life, including my struggles and troubles and all the junk I thought I could hide. I felt so free, and finally, so loved!

"Your will be done, Lord!" I told Him. But being all in for Jesus also required that I be willing to be uncomfortable on His behalf, and as the saying goes, "old habits die hard."

I am so thankful that God has never been content to ignore me and leave things as they are between us. Looking back, I can't even count the times He was knocking on my door, ready to tell me that He'd never abandon me, He could never ignore me, He loves me too much. I was never on my own—even when I thought I was hiding. Yet sometimes I have a hard time believing this.

> I am so thankful that God has never been content to ignore me and leave things as they are between us.

God has shown me tender grace, regardless of how hard I make my exterior and no matter how many times I joke about my circumstances in order to keep the focus off of me. This is my standard approach to pain: I either seize up or flippantly brush it away. And my friends can attest: this is still my go-to response when things get uncomfortable.

When I was asked to write this book, it took me more than a year to actually get on board with it, even though I felt the Lord prompting me to do it. Over an internet meeting a week ago, I even tried talking the publishers out of it. Michael Ross, who was also on this call, started to pray. I chuckle at this because of how many times he's had to do this for me. Don't you just need those praying friends?

All kinds of fearful thoughts were swirling around my head: *I have a twelfth-grade education . . . I don't have the time . . . God's going to leave me . . . I'm going to let people down, and no one will like it . . . I just want to be invisible!*

This is my brain's "muscle memory." You see, my books may give you the impression that I have it all figured out. But in reality, I'm a ridiculous self-doubter, and my feet are constantly tripping over this same obstacle.

And in those tough moments I hear God asking me the same question I asked of Cupcake: "Cara, don't you know Me by now?"

How about you? Is there an obstacle in your path that keeps tripping you up? Do you hear God asking you that same question?

I can relate, and I can also tell you that things can get better with time. At least I am done believing that God is going to leave me and that I'll end up having to figure things out on my own.

I know God personally, and He is never going to advocate for self-reliance. He wants me right where I am, completely dependent on Him.

After all God has done for me, He's not going anywhere.

And aren't we all just works in progress? God and I have done this trust dance so many times now we're almost in sync. Sure, I still doubt my worth, but I choose to walk forward anyway because I've made the choice to let Him lead this cha-cha called life.

God gives us grace for the things we trip over, and we have to be willing to purposely keep moving forward even when our muscle memory reacts. Because once you learn who God truly is, that flight-or-fight reaction is just a response to a lie.

God doesn't want us frozen in place. He wants us to make the conscious choice to keep moving forward, to keep on blazing toward the finish line, believing that He'll be there to catch us so we won't fall.

....

Lord, I so desperately want to experience Your love and to take refuge in it. Help me to turn away from worldly lies and to begin living in truth. Help me to let go of self-reliance and to surrender myself fully to You. I want to sense Your joy and peace in my life and to share that joy with others. Amen.

2

BAPTIZED AND SET FREE

Wash yourselves; make yourselves clean;
remove the evil of your doings
from before my eyes;
cease to do evil,
learn to do good;
seek justice,
rescue the oppressed,
defend the orphan,
plead for the widow.
ISAIAH 1:16–17 NRSV

As a teen Dillon was consumed by hatred toward his father. Sure, he enjoyed riding horses together and competing in rodeos with him. But once they'd return home, his dad would start drinking. He wouldn't stop until he passed out. Dillon longed for a normal family.

One day, a Christian cowboy who often competed at the rodeos showed Dillon a different way to live. He gave him a Bible—and some encouraging words.

"You look like you're having a tough day, son," the cowboy told him. "I'm here to tell you that everything's going to be okay. I know someone who picks us up, dusts us off, and gives us the strength to keep going. His name is Jesus."

In the days and weeks that followed, Dillon read his Bible and studied the life and words of Jesus. He started out with the book of James. He wanted to learn about wisdom and how to better control his temper. Then he turned to Proverbs. Before he knew it, he was learning all this cool stuff. *This book is amazing!* he thought. God pulled Dillon closer to Him.

A few months later he was ready to take action. He decided that he was giving his life to God and that he would do whatever it took to serve God's kingdom. He got baptized in a stock tank at the San Antonio Rodeo, of all places.

When he came up out of the water, he felt a massive release of everything. There was no more weight on his shoulders. Dillon stood in the cold water, shivering and completely soaked. Yet it was the best moment of his life.

> I know someone who picks us up, dusts us off, and gives us the strength to keep going. His name is Jesus.

On maps of the ancient world, cartographers always printed an arrow pointing to true north. Even if there were no east, west, or south enjoined to the symbol, the arrow and the large N would indicate the right direction to keep travelers oriented—with the invaluable assistance of a compass.

When we come to Christ, as Dillon did, God places a compass of sorts in our hearts: "If you love me, keep my commands. And I will ask the Father, and he will give you another advocate to help you and be with you forever—the Spirit of truth. The world cannot accept him, because it neither sees him nor knows him. But you know him, for he lives with you and will be in you. I will not leave you as orphans; I will come to you" (John 14:15–18).

WISDOM FROM THE HORSE FARM

The Holy Spirit sets us free
from the bondage of sin,
fills us with God's goodness,
and directs our steps.

Jesus changes us with the presence of His Holy Spirit—the Counselor who works deep inside us as our comforter, compass, and guide. He constantly points us toward His heart—our true north. And He transforms us, as Dillon discovered, from the inside out.

We experienced our own "little bit by little bit" scenario with our resident pound puppy, Abby, that we adopted from a local animal rescue a couple of years ago. I'll admit, she's spoiled. She's a very sweet girl and an obedient companion, so it's easy to go overboard on the treats with her. I'm not sure how her life was before we met, but I do know it wasn't great. So maybe that's why it's so fulfilling to expose her to a life that is the complete opposite of the one she had before.

This past summer I stopped in at one of my favorite butcher shops, and without embarrassment I will admit that I purchased a pound of beef sticks (with cheese) for Abby as a treat. Well, now that I'm putting this to paper, I'm a little embarrassed. But hey, I love my dog.

When I got home I was so excited to give her a meat stick. She took it from my hand, but about five minutes later I found her in the corner with the meat stick at her feet and with a strange look on her face.

Because she wasn't used to such lavish gifts, she had concluded that my gift was too good to be true, and she was suspicious. She looked at me as if to say, "So what's the catch?"

If we are used to life being one way and then we witness the life of someone following Jesus, we think it's too good to be true. Before I became a Christ-follower, I used to look at these types of do-gooders and think they must want something.

In Abby's case I had to break that meat stick into pieces for her to accept the gift, or as Dillon's story goes, I fed her a little bit, a little bit, a little bit.

I have met believers who wrestle with God because they feel that they've done everything the right way, to no avail. Here they are, going to church every week and living a good Christian life, and then something

horrible happens to them. Because their circumstances do not fit what they feel they deserve from God, they struggle with unmet expectations.

Just the opposite of that, I spent the first year of my conversion waiting for something to go wrong or to be punished by God. Not because of unmet expectations by God but rather because I knew I was a loser and I didn't deserve the gift of salvation. It was too good to be true.

How could I be lovable to God when I had been so unlovable?

But God doesn't love us because we're lovable or because we make Him feel good. He loves us because He is love.

Like Dillon, I had to take it in slowly, until one morning, while having coffee with my friend Beamon, I had the overwhelming feeling that I needed to be baptized. No stock tank was available, so Beamon took his cowboy boots off and dunked me in the swimming pool, and I came up reborn, facing north.

Jesus didn't come to earth to make my life better. Jesus came to save my life.

Jesus gives our lives direction. How to live, how to forgive, and how to love others. He asks us to believe first, then see. He asks us to trust that such a lavish gift is ours for the taking and with no caveats.

Before I became a Christ-follower, I used to look at these types of do-gooders and think they must want something.

Recently, my friend Brandon started playing guitar. It had seemed overwhelming at first. "But I practice a little every day," he told me, "and every day I get a little bit better."

Better today than yesterday.

This applies to our Christian walk as well. If we spend time in God's Word a little every day (even if we can muster only five minutes), we will keep growing closer to Jesus all the way to the finish line.

Lord, thank You for cleansing my soul and setting me free. Thank You for Your grace. Thank You for being patient with me while I learned to draw closer to You. You forgive . . . and then give so much back. Help me to trust more, to change what needs to be changed, to grow, and to serve You. Amen.

3

"I BELIEVE IN MIRACLES"

I pray that God, who gives hope, will bless you with
complete happiness and peace because of your faith. And
may the power of the Holy Spirit fill you with hope.
ROMANS 15:13 CEV

ithin two short years Erin walked through the "the valley of the shadow of death" twice—first losing her unborn baby, Mike, and then her mother. Her heart was crushed, and her faith had taken a beating. Yet just hours before her mother's passing, Erin's mom shared something miraculous: She talked about seeing Jesus. "He has hair on His face," Erin's mom told her. "Just a little. And He wears a crown that is bright. He is good . . . and His hands are taking away my cancer and my pain. Oh, how I really, really love those hands!"

Erin's mom died five days before Erin's birthday. Her mother had loved celebrating each child's special day—always wanting to be the first to say, "Happy Birthday!" At 2:00 a.m., just a couple of hours into Erin's big day, her two-year-old daughter, Paisley, came into her room, gently tugged on her arm, and then made an announcement that caused Erin to bolt out of bed: "Grandma came into my dream and told me to wake you up and wish you happy birthday. She said she loves heaven. Oh, and she told me that she is taking care of baby Mike, so you don't have to worry about him! Good night, Mommy."

Tears rolled down Erin's cheeks. *Baby Mike?!* she thought. *Oh, dear Lord, You are amazing. Your love comforts us at just the right moment—and You never cease to deliver one miracle after another!*

Erin's thoughts flashed to the dark valleys she and her husband had walked through over the past several months . . . and all the "why" questions that rolled through her mind over and over. Yes, her heart was broken, yet she hadn't lost her faith. And in reality, God was blessing her. "I'm choosing to keep putting one step ahead of the other," she prayed out loud. "And I'll continue to seek You through the crushing moments as well as the good ones. You're healing my heart—just as You've taken away my mom's pain. And I know I'll get to see her and my sweet baby someday. I know Mike is well cared for. Thank You, Jesus. *Thank You!*"

One of her mother's dying wishes was that Erin would have a baby boy. On July 23, 2019, Erin and her husband welcomed Jeter David into the world. Their boy—and the very child her mother had prayed for just a week before she passed into eternity.

Erin still smiles when she imagines the joy on her mother's face whenever she would talk to her about heaven. Even though their time together was cut short, Erin felt as if she had gained a lifetime of wisdom from her mom. And through her mother's death, Erin has received an eternal focus. Today, she's convinced that eternity isn't that far off for any of us. "The space between this life and heaven is very thin," she insists. "It's almost palpable."

WISDOM
FROM THE
HORSE FARM

The Holy Spirit heals our
pain and fills us with joy.

The Lord pulled my friend out of despair and filled her heart with joy and wonder. For Erin, it was her amazing "God encounters" that changed everything.

"All of these events have built my faith," Erin told me. "I believe in miracles. I have seen them with my own eyes. I believe in heaven. My mom is there with our sweet baby boy Mike and with so many other loved ones."

Her story has shown me the difference between being broken and being blessed.

I first met Erin a few years ago when I became middle-aged enough to start pulling muscles in my sleep. She is one of the most tender people I know, and she's both a physical therapist and a Pilates instructor. I decided to start Pilates training with her as a way to become stronger and more limber. I thought, *Hey, if I ever slip and fall, I can use my new strong and limber body to avoid breaking something.*

And being who I am—an evangelist—I also thought this would also be a great opportunity to witness to someone new.

When I walked into the Pilates studio for the first time and met Erin, she was surrounded by bouquets of flowers. "Is it your birthday?" I asked.

As it turned out it was actually the one-year anniversary of her mom's passing, so the flowers were there to cheer her up. As she put it, "I have great friends."

It got me thinking as I started my stretching routine: *Maybe God put me here to be a witness and to give her some encouragement.*

As I started my usual prying into her personal spiritual life (nope, I just can't help myself), I quickly concluded that Erin was a follower of Jesus. A strong one. And before you could say, "Let's do the Hundred,

followed by the Criss-Cross and Single-Leg Circles," the tables had turned. Erin became an encouragement to me. A big one.

Her faith journey reminded me that Jesus still allows us to witness and to participate in His miracles. And her testimony is so healing. It's such a blessing to those of us who wait with broken hearts to be reunited with those who have gone before us into eternity.

Erin's story takes my mind back to the farm and how God used a horse to show me the difference between being broken and being blessed. It's a reminder that all will be healed and restored at the end of this race.

What's the difference between breaking a horse and training one?

About eight years ago I purchased a horse that I didn't understand. I liked him; then I didn't like him. And I'm almost positive he didn't like me. I just could not figure out what made Gus tick. A friend of mine recommended that I take him to a barn where an old cowboy named Smokey taught natural horsemanship methods. Together with Smokey, I learned how to speak the language of horse.

I asked Smokey where he'd learned this magic method, assuming that, much like in the movies, he had some wild story, like he was raised on horse milk and ran off to live on the range among the wild stallions, like Jane Goodall with chimpanzees, but with equines instead. But no such story existed. To my surprise Smokey told me that natural horse-manship was actually very new to him. Up until the last decade, he'd done it his dad's way: the old cowboy method of using fear and pain to break the horse's will into submission.

Smokey recalled a time when he saw his dad on top of a horse. His dad was pulling the reins tight, and the horse had blood coming out its mouth. He remembered times that his dad withheld food or left a horse tied up for hours. By basically dominating the horse with fear and pain, Smokey's dad would psychologically get it to a place where it no longer wanted to buck, bolt, or rear.

I'm so thankful after hearing these stories that there is another way to get our horses to a place of compliance. I would rather have Gus's respect and confidence than for him to be afraid of me.

During that year that I worked with Gus and with Smokey, I fell in love with Gus. I learned to understand what Gus was trying to tell me the whole time. I could read in his eyes when Gus had hit his threshold for the day, and Gus learned that I could be trusted.

I could tell Gus with my presence, "I'm going to put pressure on you, friend, so you know what I am asking you to do. But you can still trust that this is what's best for you. I am your safe place, Gus. I am where you find your rest."

Over time, Gus and I formed a partnership. A true and genuine union.

Like the cowboys of old, those hard "whys" of life try to capture and break us. We bolt, and we try to dodge all the problems of this world so they don't catch us. We buck and we rear because even though we are made in the image of God, we were also created with these wild human hearts. Although God isn't obligated to give us an answer to our life questions, He does train us through them to achieve a true and genuine union with each of us individually.

Jesus is our mentor. He is the Way.

> Like the cowboys of old, those hard "whys" of life try to capture and break us. We bolt, and we try to dodge all the problems of this world.

He shows us how He submitted to God and asks us to do the same. He is the pioneer and the perfecter of faith. Jesus doesn't try to break us with cruelty or intimidation. Instead, He tells us, "Do not be afraid." He wants our wild hearts to submit to Him willingly; He wants us to bring our trauma, and He will train it into hope.

Jesus trains us to be strong and limber so we can carry on His work here on earth. While we run toward our eternal home, we can use our training to proclaim the gospel. His sweet assurance that miracles happen. His promise that we will see our loved ones again. The message that even though we slip and fall, we will not falter, because we know all will be healed and restored at the end of this race.

That's how it is for my friend Erin.

She says the gift of eternity has given her new eyesight. She believes that every struggle, every challenge, every gift we receive is from God. Together, they allow us to shift our focus to the big picture and can remind us that no matter what we face today, the journey we are on is bringing us one step closer to eternity.

This perspective has allowed her to take risks, to love stronger, to forgive more, to quiet her mind so she can sense God working in her life. "Life is truly a gift," she added, "but I'll be honest: the gift of eternity in heaven is one that I am really looking forward to."

....

Lord, thank You for meeting me at my darkest point. Thank You for wiping away the tears and restoring my hope. Now let me use Your example of love to shine some light into a darkened world. Amen.

4

THE LONELY RIDE

For God so loved the world that he gave his one and only
Son, that whoever believes in him shall not perish but have
eternal life. For God did not send his Son into the world
to condemn the world, but to save the world through him.
Whoever believes in him is not condemned, but whoever
does not believe stands condemned already because they
have not believed in the name of God's one and only Son.

JOHN 3:16–18

Ashley's life felt like a long, lonely ride along an uncertain trail. She knew she had to give God the reins and trust Him with each step—at least, that's what her heart was telling her to do. Common sense, on the other hand, was shouting something entirely different: "Retreat . . . *now!* Get off the trail and run the other way!"

Her path had been filled with unthinkable twists and turns, not to mention a sheer drop-off that she knew she could tumble down with just one misstep.

And the way ahead didn't look any easier.

"Lord, I trust You," she whispered, keeping her eyes focused on each step. "I'm barely holding on, and I don't understand all these challenges . . . but I'll keep trusting You."

Ashley remembered a time when she wasn't able to say those words.

Growing up, she and her family were what some would describe as "holiday Christians." She had been baptized as a baby and had recited nightly prayers as a little girl—"Now I lay me down to sleep . . ."—yet that was the extent of her religious experience.

Fast-forward to age nineteen, when she met a young man who would later become her husband. "Come to church with me," he prompted.

"No," Ashley responded. "That's not my thing. I'm not religious."

"Neither am I. It's about faith; it's about Jesus."

Ashley squinted for a moment, gazing at the handsome boy standing before her, and then she smiled. "Sure," she said, "I can do that."

It didn't take long for Ashley to feel a strange pull in her heart, a tug like she had never felt. Still, she constantly struggled with the how and why of faith and was hungry for proof.

Ashley eventually married that boy who'd invited her to church, and the two had three beautiful daughters. At last, Ashley was living the charmed life she'd always wanted. Yet in an instant, the rug was pulled out from under her.

"I've noticed that my youngest daughter just isn't developing typically," she told a pediatrician during a routine visit. Her instincts told her that something was wrong.

Weeks later, Ashley's fears were confirmed when a team of experts told her that her child may never walk . . . or talk.

"I wish we had answers for you, but we don't," her doctor said. "We simply don't know exactly what's causing the delay in her development."

Ashley thought of Psalm 139:14, where King David wrote, "I praise you because I am fearfully and wonderfully made; your works are wonderful, I know that full well." Shouldn't her baby be perfect too?

Suddenly, many of the verses Ashley had read in her Bible were making her angry. She felt mad at God—confused and beginning to doubt His plan. She even doubted God Himself.

"I don't feel His presence," Ashley told her husband. "I feel alone and forgotten."

"He's there," her husband told her. "We don't always feel His presence, but He hasn't left us. We've got to keep praying . . . and hoping."

One night, when she had reached the end of her rope, encouragement she had received from her husband and friends flashed through her mind: "It's about faith; it's about Jesus."

So, she got on her knees and cried out to God: "I don't sense You in my life, and I don't understand Your ways . . . but I believe You are there. I need You, Lord."

Ashley let God in and felt Him in a way she had never experienced before.

"The pain we were experiencing was countered by peace and absolute joy at what He was trusting *us* with," she told a friend later. "I asked Jesus to come into my heart and have been tug-of-warring with Him ever since. It hasn't been easy, but I know He is real."

Today Ashley does her best to release the reins to God—trusting that He will protect her from the uncertain twists and turns and sheer drop-offs.

Her daughter does, in fact, walk and talk, but she is intellectually disabled and has developed epilepsy and other issues that keep Ashley in a constant state of anxiety. Her child has needs that will require her to live with Ashley through adulthood. "But she's also precious, and radiates joy, makes us laugh, and is always smiling."

Ashley's older daughters have had to grow up much faster—they've had to see and take on things that most adults don't experience. But they're also witness to God's work in each of us. "We've all been forced to be selfless, tender, caring, and flexible," Ashley says. "Characteristics we may not necessarily have if God had not given us this special little girl. He reminds me almost daily of the pure *joy* that we see through our daughter and continues to give us peace and protection over her."

I wonder sometimes why God tells us no when other paths seem so well lit and easier. How can we accept the will of our Father when He allows us to struggle along a bumpy, murky road with no visible patterns?

That's how it was for my friend Ashley.

If you'd like to learn how I met her, I invite you to read the last chapter in my previous book, *Fields of Grace*. I think God always meant for us to be friends. I walked alongside Ashley as best I could during her darkest times, and I will admit, I asked God why it seemed as if He was thwarting her dreams. How could a loving God allow this much chaos in my friend's life? Ashley and I both find comfort in control, but there was none. I cried out to my Lord and made grand petitions on her behalf.

"Give me some of Ashley's burden. Give it to me, Lord! Because I am scared that she will leave You!" I prayed desperately that she would have a road-to-Damascus moment. "Let Ashley see You, Lord!" I could only

WISDOM
FROM THE
HORSE FARM

The Holy Spirit turns our
hearts toward God and opens
our minds to the truth.

hope that this spiral of chaotic events was meant to draw my friend closer to Him.

But here's the beauty in the ashes: a person with true faith sticks around, not only when life tosses you from your expected patterns but also after that hell-bound piece of worthless trash the devil burns your barn to the ground.

Because we know God *will* rebuild it. We believers live it as fact.

Like Ashley, as believers we believe everything—and I mean *everything*—will be made perfect at the end of this race. Ashley knew that the whole time; she believed it. Even though she once told me, "I can't feel God in any of this." And even after saying, "It doesn't feel like God even cares," she still chose to believe that God tells the truth. Feelings and disappointments can get the better of us, so we have to lean on what we know to be true all the way to the finish line. Believe me when I say there are actually a few things God can't do: He cannot lie and He cannot deceive us. God is good, and we trust His Word even when we can't see the pattern or make sense of the route.

We have to come to lean on what we know to be true. Because emotions make for a shaky faith, and although feelings are essential, on occasions we need to make the conscious choice to put them under.

....

Lord, as Scripture tells us, "God did not send his Son into the world to condemn the world, but to save the world through him. Whoever believes in him is not condemned." Thank You for Your gift of everlasting life . . . and the strength to believe. Transform my heart. Draw me closer to You. Amen.

5

GENTLE HANDS, HUGGABLE HORSES

I know what it is to have little, and I know what
it is to have plenty. In any and all circumstances I
have learned the secret of being well-fed and of going
hungry, of having plenty and of being in need. I can
do all things through him who strengthens me.
PHILIPPIANS 4:12–13 NRSV

Kevin brushed Dakota with long, slow, gentle strokes, and then he rubbed the horse's neck. "You are a beauty," he told the animal, "and my favorite of the herd."

Dakota leaned into his human friend, tilted his head to one side, and looked at Kevin with one eye. It was almost as if he were saying, "I like you! Keep doing what you're doing! Please, please don't stop!"

The horse was a stunner of an Appaloosa—all fifteen hands of him. His velvety, cream-colored coat was splattered with random patches of bold chestnut spots, making Kevin wonder if the animal had stepped right out of an artist's painting. And he had an adorable personality, drawing people in with authentic affection.

Because Dakota was so gentle with strangers, he served an important role as a therapy horse. And today, he'd get the chance to bring joy to a disabled teen named Katie, letting the child brush and hug him. With Kevin's guidance, the two would venture out on a peaceful trail ride through Missouri's rolling countryside.

Kevin adjusted his hat and peeked out the barn. There wasn't a cloud in the sky. "It's gonna be a scorcher today," Kevin told Dakota. "Let's get you watered and saddled up."

The horse whinnied and bobbed its head. Kevin rubbed its neck again. "Don't worry; you'll be getting a lot of that today. Katie will be here any minute!"

Twice a week, Kevin joined dozens of other volunteers at a neighbor's horse farm in Festus—just a stone's throw from his own ranch in nearby Pevely. Together, he and a team of 150 local cowboys served more than eighty children, adults, and veterans with physical or occupational needs. The equine-assisted therapy that Kevin and his friends provided was absolutely free, and it was designed to do one thing: bring smiles to people's faces. Ultimately, it strengthened their confidence.

That's how it was for Kevin, too . . . and that's what had brought him to this farm.

He'd once let a horse nuzzle its way into his own hurting heart. "These animals are so special," he'd told the farm's owner the day he decided to volunteer. "They've been there for me, nudging me through some of the hardest times of my life. That's why I'm here; that's why I'm giving back."

As Kevin prepared Dakota for a busy day, his thoughts wandered back to the pain that had brought him to this place. Struggles on the home front, coupled

> The equine-assisted therapy that Kevin and his friends provided was absolutely free, and it was designed to do one thing: bring smiles to people's faces.

with a long season spent wandering through a spiritual desert, had left Kevin doubting his faith and questioning God's plan for his life. "I feel so lost and alone, Lord," he'd pray. "I feel so numb. What's the point of my life? Where's the hope?"

Day after day, he'd catch the eye of the horses on his farm as he would brush and care for them. He felt an instant connection with the animals. He knew all too well that horses were keen observers and were vigilant and sensitive to movement and emotion. They often mirror our feelings, conveying understanding and empathy, which enables us to feel safe.

Gradually, brush stroke after brush stroke, Kevin's heart began to mend. And instead of continuing to limp along—frustrated, lonely, and feeling spiritually stuck—he learned that within his reach was the promise of a meaningful day. *Lord, I know how You're going to use this mixed-up, broken-down cowboy. And maybe I'm not as mixed-up and broken-down as I thought!*

Suddenly, the sound of a car door slamming and that familiar voice he loved so much brought Kevin back into the moment.

"Dakota, I'm here," Katie shouted.

The horse didn't bat an eye. He was busy getting a drink.

A slurping, sucking sound drowned out the world as he siphoned water through pursed lips. But once he'd got his fill, Dakota raised his head and spotted Katie . . . who immediately threw her arms around him.

Kevin adjusted his hat again and smiled. *Yep—it's going to be a great day!*

Just as God is busting down barriers in the lives of the men, women, and children Kevin serves, the Lord is delivering this seasoned cowboy from his own spiritual handicaps—things like fear and doubt, a

WISDOM FROM THE HORSE FARM

The Holy Spirit compels us to serve God and gives us exactly what we need to accomplish the Lord's work.

spiritual desert . . . and even his own misconceptions about what God can accomplish through a willing heart.

One thing's for sure: equine therapy made a difference for Kevin. In fact, research proves that it can lower a person's blood pressure and heart rate, alleviate stress, and reduce symptoms of anxiety and depression.[1] Equine therapy also helps people struggling with addictions or mental illness. And as Kevin is learning, there are several life skills that a horse can teach better than a person.

Kevin and his friends are realizing what the apostle Paul had learned when he wrote, "I can do all things through him who strengthens me" (Philippians 4:13 NRSV). But Kevin also knows that if God gave us everything we wanted the instant we asked for it, our faith would not be strengthened. We'd wrongly interpret that God was deserting us every time things didn't go our way.

"That's a lie the Enemy wants us to believe," Kevin says. "Yet God never abandons us. So, 'in any and all circumstances I have learned the secret of being well-fed and of going hungry, of having plenty and of being in need.' I am learning to keep my focus on my Lord and Savior—Jesus Christ!"

That's a lesson I'm discovering on my own farm.

About eight years ago I tried something I never thought I would have any interest in. I tried my hand at carriage driving. To be honest, I had a horse that I really wasn't sure what to do with. Gus, who I mentioned in an earlier chapter, was a big and bulky Norwegian Fjord Horse. He was well-behaved but didn't seem to enjoy being ridden at all. So, I investigated carriage driving, found Gus and myself an instructor, and discovered that

Gus really preferred pulling. He was made for it! And I discovered that I really enjoyed navigating Gus and the carriage through sets of cones during obstacle classes.

"Driving cones" is all about focus. We found out pretty quickly the trick was to aim for the center of the space between the cones; get Gus properly lined up; change my focus to a spot past the set of cones, straight out ahead of me; then maintain this focus until Gus and the carriage were all the way through the set of cones.

My trainer would say, "Remember: do not look down at the cones as you drive through!" If our focus wavered before Gus and the carriage were all the way through, we would most likely hit a cone—exactly what we were trying to avoid.

All in all, Gus and I made a pretty good driving team, and although we didn't take home many ribbons despite our trying, our experience was purposeful. We deepened our friendship, and Gus was more content to be paid in fruit than with trophies. I always made sure there was a ripe red apple at the end of each obstacle course.

A few years later, Gus developed eye cysts, and even though I was able to take care of most of his eyesight issues with surgery at the Iowa State University Medical Center, he would no longer wear his blinkers or pull his carriage. We both retired from driving, and as I write these words, my good friend Gustafson is enjoying a nap under a clear blue Nebraska sky.

Kevin's story shows us that there isn't a Christ-follower alive who is immune to spiritual struggles. Sometimes, we experience moments when we don't sense God in our lives, so we begin to doubt ourselves . . . even our faith. It can happen to anyone at any time. And while there is much to be learned in these deserts, we've got to regain our focus and get back to the place where God has called us to be.

We are told to run our race with our eyes focused on Christ. Kevin reminds us not to look down at the cones that catch our side vision. False idols, like alcohol, chewing tobacco, sports, work, music, video games, and TV, are like those cones, and they can take our focus off Jesus. Did you realize that? An idol can be a person, a pursuit—anything that takes priority over Jesus. And if we don't allow the Lord to direct our steps, we can end up living like an idolater—without even realizing it. These things can keep us from opening and reading the Bible, having an abundant prayer life, and recognizing our dependence on Jesus.

So, what things rule your life? What is holding you back? Are you learning to trust Christ . . . and to take a step of faith with Him every day? Do you yearn for a greater level of spiritual intimacy with Jesus?

As we read about Kevin refocusing on Jesus, we see how Jesus led him out of a desert filled with doubt and emptiness and gave him the confidence to accomplish far more than he'd ever imagined.

God knows we all have fears and concerns about our abilities. And just as Kevin is discovering, He is training us for something better, something that requires us to learn to trust in Him. God has a firm grip on the lead rope. He will guide us where we need to be.

Just keep your eyes off those cones!

....

Lord, I'm so thankful that I can do all things through You, who strengthens me. Teach me to find contentment in my circumstances, and give me the courage to step out in faith. Show me that I can do infinitely more than I ever thought possible. Amen.

PART 2

God's Spirit Makes Us Peaceful and Patient

6

WALKING, WAITING . . . RUNNING

Rejoice in the Lord always; again I will say, Rejoice.
Let your gentleness be known to everyone. The Lord is
near. Do not worry about anything, but in everything
by prayer and supplication with thanksgiving let your
requests be made known to God. And the peace of
God, which surpasses all understanding, will guard
your hearts and your minds in Christ Jesus.
PHILIPPIANS 4:4–7 NRSV

aiting. Debra was not good at it, and she didn't like it. The worst thing about receiving a life-threatening diagnosis is waiting.

Waiting for results, waiting for surgery, waiting for more results, waiting to talk to doctors, waiting for results again, waiting to start treatment, waiting to see if the treatment worked. *Waiting!*

Debra accepted Christ when she was twelve while at a Bible camp in western Nebraska. Her faith in Jesus was a part of her life from then on. She knew she was never alone in her Christian walk, though there have been life challenges that would classify as crisis-of-faith experiences.

One such experience happened more than a decade ago when she was diagnosed with breast cancer at age forty-seven. No one can prepare you for those words, "You have cancer." As the doctor walked out of the room to give her and her husband a minute to process, the tears began to fall. Hundreds of questions swirled through Debra's mind: *What will the future hold? How bad is it? When can I schedule surgery? How will we tell the kids? Will I see them grow up?*

More waiting.

Once surgery had been officially scheduled for the following week, the reality of her circumstances set in and anxiety began to overtake Debra. Suddenly, she couldn't eat, she couldn't sleep, and she was growing unusually quiet and withdrawn—not usual for her.

One day, as she sat alone with her thoughts, she sensed God asking her a critical question: *"Do you trust Me?"*

Debra leaned back and groaned. More tears rolled down her cheeks. "If I can be completely honest, Lord," she prayed, "no, I don't. I want to trust You, but I just don't."

Once her surgery was behind her and she was into the long weeks of recovery, doctors decided that she would need four rounds of chemo and six weeks of radiation.

Radiation . . . ugh!

While her cancer was caught early and her prognosis was good, Debra wasn't leaping for joy just yet. And quiet moment after quiet moment, she sensed God asking her that same question: *"Do you trust Me?"*

Still, "No."

Let's see how this thing turns out, Debra thought. *Can it be that my cancer experience is the litmus test of whether I believe God is deserving of my trust?*

Debra wrestled with her thoughts again, this time staring at a cold, stark chemo room. It wasn't the picture of joy and encouragement that she so desperately needed at that moment. Instead, it was a large space set up with recliners, each occupied by a quiet, expressionless individual receiving IV chemo treatment. As Debra received her first dose, two thoughts rattled around her brain: *What am I doing here?* and *This is not my life!*

At one moment she looked up and caught her husband, Dan's, gaze. He smiled, then opened a book sitting on his lap. It was *Fearless* by Max Lucado. Dan began to read out loud:

> When fear shapes our lives, safety becomes our god. When safety becomes our god, we worship the risk-free life. Can the safety lover do anything great? Can the risk-averse accomplish noble deeds? For God? For others? No. The fear-filled cannot love deeply; love is risky. They cannot give to the poor. Benevolence has no guarantee of return. The fear-filled cannot dream wildly. What if their dreams sputter and fall from the sky? The worship of safety emasculates greatness. No wonder Jesus wages such a war against fear.[2]

Then Dan looked his wife in the eyes and said this: "Everyone here is going through the same thing you are, so we are going to bring hope into this chemo room."

As Debra's husband continued to read, she closed her eyes and prayed. *God, I'm scared. God, I don't know what the future holds. God, I want to see my children grow up. God, help me trust You despite the circumstances.*

"I don't know how to describe the feeling of peace that overtook my spirit as God began to show Himself to me in ways I had never experienced before," Debra later told her husband.

"When fear shapes our lives, safety becomes our god."
Max Lucado

In spite of her distrust, the Lord showed Himself to be trustworthy in more ways than Debra could count. He amazed her with His love and patience for her as He brought person after person to Debra during her cancer journey. People who lifted her up, prayed for her, and increased her faith in Him. He gave her the strength to walk boldly in her journey, and He gave her multiple opportunities to share her story and her faith walk as she battled cancer. And on those days post chemo when all she could do was lie on the couch, unable to do much but rest, the Lord calmed her anxious heart and whispered to her, *"I have a plan for you, but you will have to wait. Do you trust Me?"*

Waiting again. That wasn't easy for Debra, but she knew she could trust the Lord, so okay, she'd wait.

Dan continued reading during her chemo treatments. He shared the hope of Jesus with Debra and all those who could hear in that chemo room. God gave Debra peace through it all, unexplainable peace that could only have come from Him. He also gave her opportunities to share her faith when she was asked, "How do you have such a good outlook on life in this?"

Over the next year the Lord gave Debra the privilege to walk four other women through their cancer journeys—and was herself healed. She prayed with them, cried with them, and showed the love and peace of Jesus with them.

Debra just celebrated her ten-year anniversary of being cancer-free. While she doesn't want to have a repeat experience with cancer, God used that time in her life to show her truths about Himself that she might not have been open to hear under any other circumstance.

God is still refining her heart, she says, calming her anxiousness when she goes to her cancer checkups . . . and the Lord is still asking her to wait on Him for the future.

"I have seen Him be faithful time and time again as He has shown me His trustworthiness even when I doubted Him," Debra says.

Is it possible to walk and wait at the same time? When it comes to horses, you get the most out of your relationship with your four-legged friends if you can teach them to walk and wait at the same time.

All horses, especially those that are meant to perform in an arena, can get to the place where they stop waiting and listening for your cues, especially if they think they already know the pattern you want them to travel. They will step ahead of your instruction, anticipating your next move. And although your horse can get it right some of the time, it can never predict it correctly all the time.

Once there is a change to your standard routine, suddenly the horse has a hard time adjusting and trusting that you are in control. Your horse will no longer be willfully guided because you've put a change in your standard routine without its say-so.

Running the same patterns in the practice arena over and over again or doing the same warm-ups before a show makes for a dishonest relationship between you and your horse because your pony will only be going through the motions and not really listening to what you are asking of it. To avoid this, you need to mix running your horse through the same paces daily with teaching it some new movements.

In our lives we can sometimes fall into the same circles, lead changes,

WISDOM
FROM THE
HORSE FARM

The Holy Spirit restores peace
and sets our minds on truth.

and stops. But God allows for things that we can't predict. Life doesn't always follow the same sequence and make sense, and that's because God wants to keep us honest. That's why it's important to learn how to wait as we are walking with God. Yes, it's possible for us to keep moving ahead and also wait while we are doing it. God used Debra's circumstance to teach her how to both walk and wait.

I met Deb when she was the guidance counselor at my children's school. When I made the decision to home-school my kids in a group of other like-minded parents, I just figured she was a person who would be in my sphere one day and not the next. Life demonstrates to us the many times that people can come in and out of our lives, but God is funny about sisterhood. He eventually laid a big ask on Deb's heart. Deb came into our homeschool group as a teacher.

> Life doesn't always follow the same sequence and make sense, and that's because God wants to keep us honest.

By then she had been cancer-free for a time. But I will tell you, I see the fear behind her eyes when she has to make her way to Omaha for her routine oncology checkups. I have been told multiple times by cancer survivors that every time you head to checkups, the same fears come flooding back into your chest. So, we grit our teeth, and we pray, and we wait.

I asked Deb to contribute to this chapter because I knew that what she had to say would benefit so many people who have had to walk through a season of illness. We can only guess why God has instructed so many to walk with Him and to trust Him in the waiting. Perhaps it is only to say, "I need to keep you listening to Me and not so reliant on your own say-so."

I can't even count how many times I've anticipated God's next move in my own life and tried to "help Him along" by making a decision before

His almighty say-so. Sometimes I get it right and sometimes I am not even close to predicting what God was up to. His way is always the most loving way to go.

You would never put your horse in the position to start making decisions on its own. And God will never put us in a position to make our own decisions without the guidance of His Holy Spirit. Our goal should be to not let our minds run ahead into the arena of what-ifs.

What a blessing it is to see that waiting is possible through Jesus' own race. As we watch His ministry unfold in the Bible, we read about Jesus as He waits for His "time" to come.

He waits to be betrayed, waits to be flogged, and waits to die.

His disciples wait three days in despair. *But* we watch Him rise again! It's definitely worth the wait. And it changes everything.

Deb and Dan show us that while it's difficult to wait and run, it's not impossible when you know that Jesus has already blazed a similar race before you, and as we study how Jesus did it, we learn to trust Him.

Lord, please fill me with the peace that only You can give. Help me to rest in Your love and warm embrace as I walk through this day. With a thankful heart, I trust in You. Amen.

7

THE PATIENT GARDENER

Be patient, then, brothers and sisters, until the
Lord's coming. See how the farmer waits for the land
to yield its valuable crop, patiently waiting for the
autumn and spring rains. You too, be patient and
stand firm, because the Lord's coming is near.
JAMES 5:7–8

Kim adjusted her hat, wiped sweat off her brow, and surveyed the most sacred part of her home: a sprawling garden just off her kitchen.

In every direction explosions of color dazzled her eyes: purple irises, yellow daffodils, pink dahlia, and red tulips. Giving shade to her masterpiece were three towering oak trees she had planted years earlier. All her hard work was paying off—the constant watering, weeding, and pruning, not to mention the endless hours of patience just wondering if anything was going to take root and grow.

As Kim sat comfortably on a bench positioned right in the middle of her sanctuary, she noticed something at her feet—a wooden box with several small bags of seed organized neatly inside. She reached down and pulled out a couple of packets. One read "oak," the other "crocus." The seeds inside looked the same: small, brown, and seemingly lifeless. *Yet this is how it all begins,* she told herself. *The potential inside each one of these seeds is infinitely different.*

Kim couldn't help thinking that it's the same with people—and with our faith. God has given us life with a blueprint. He knows our potential, our stories, and our impact on others because He created us. There is a seed of faith inside each of us that God is nurturing, watering, fertilizing, and growing.

> There is a seed of faith inside each of us that God is nurturing, watering, fertilizing, and growing.

Her mind flashed to her four teenage children—each so unique yet deeply connected by the bonds of faith and family. *So far, I'm raising an engineer, an athlete, a caregiver, and a pastor,* Kim thought to herself. *Yep—my little seeds are blossoming into such different people . . . and each one is serving God in their own way.*

The fifty-something Missourian picked up her Bible and flipped through the pages. "I think God's Word has a lot to say about this," she said to herself, and then began to read aloud: "For we are his workmanship, created in Christ Jesus for good works, which God prepared beforehand, that we should walk in them" (ESV).

She clicked a pen, underlined the verse—Ephesians 2:10—and jotted a note in the margin: *If we're patient and steadfast, and if we trust God's blueprint by following Him, we'll grow into the exact Jesus-reflecting, God-serving, kingdom-building people He created us to be.*

Kim found another verse and stuck her finger on the page to hold it, flipped through a few more pages, and landed on a third passage of Scripture. Then she read each line and jotted more notes in the margins of her Bible:

So then neither the one who plants nor the one who waters is anything, but God who causes the growth. (1 Corinthians 3:7 NASB)

Now that you have purified yourselves by obeying the truth so that you have sincere love for each other, love one another deeply, from the heart. For you have been born again, not of perishable seed, but of imperishable, through the living and enduring word of God. For, "All people are like grass, and all their glory is like the flowers of the field; the grass withers and the flowers fall, but the word of the Lord endures forever." (1 Peter 1:22–25)

Kim wrote frantically—the words flowing from her heart:

We each have the ability to bear different kinds of fruit through the Holy Spirit. The fruit we bear provides new seeds that can be sown. What kinds of seeds? A loving act of kindness we share, a sweet prayer, a friendly smile. All these "giving-of-yourself" types of seeds vary by each person and each situation. But once they are sown, they can produce quite a plentiful harvest. The key is a patient, steadfast faith.

Kim closed her Bible, adjusted her hat again, and smiled as she took one last look at the sprawling garden before her. *Time to get moving. Time to serve the patient Gardener.*

Christ-followers become better, happier, and more loving when they discover their God-given purpose and use it to impact others for God's eternal kingdom. It's wise to accept that we're each a "bulb" and not an "acorn" . . . or in my case, a Nebraska farmer and not a Wall Street guru. We don't have to change how God made us. I need to be a "humble seed"

WISDOM FROM THE HORSE FARM

The Holy Spirit gives us patience as we pursue God's plans.

and allow the Lord to grow me into the unique person He planned for me to be.

We are who God made us to be, and the same thing can be said about our critters.

Think about how many horses, dogs, cats, fish, turtles, and birds you have owned and how they each have had their own unique quirks, funny habits, favorite toys, and preferred foods. On my farm one horse likes green apples and refuses to eat red. And just yesterday, we were laughing at our dog Abby, who has this hilarious quirk: the dog growls at Grandma Shirley when she stops petting her.

I have owned many dogs since childhood, and I can confidently say that while some are similar, no two of them were *exactly* alike. The same can be said of God's people.

Remember the packets of seeds Kim stores in the wooden box under her bench? As I imagine each one, I can't help thinking about all the potential locked into each one. But here's what gets me most excited: God knows what those seeds will become. Likewise, He knows every intimate detail of our lives, He loves us just as we are, and He connects with us in unique ways. We read in the Bible how He spoke personally to everyone He encountered. Jesus had a completely different conversation with the Samaritan woman than He did with Nicodemus or the crippled beggar.

The Lord spoke with people about spiritual issues right where they were and in ways they could understand. And that's a good example for us to follow. Since most people feel more at ease around those who share their interests, finding common ground can open opportunities for spiritual seeds to be planted. And as we make personal connections with others and water each seed—in other words, as we spend time with them and share God's love with those we meet—we may even get to watch their faith bloom right before our eyes.

Many people make the commitment to follow Jesus but then feel as if they are expected to change some aspect of their personality. I know I felt that pressure too. Yet in reality God wants each of us to be exactly who we are—the special, one-of-a-kind person He created us to be.

So, when we make the commitment to follow Jesus, that doesn't mean we become Christian clones, listening to one style of music, wearing one style of clothing, or hanging out with people who look and talk a certain way. While I use my God-given talents to write Christian books, I sometimes feel the need to rock out to one of my favorite musicians, Alice Cooper. I've always been a fan of his music, and perhaps you and I have that in common. This is something that makes us unique. Surprisingly, Alice Cooper is a Christ-follower. What a great witness he must be to the rock stars around him who travel in his sphere of influence.

> God wants each of us to be exactly who we are—the special, one-of-a-kind person He created us to be.

Yes, we must repent of our sin . . . and, yes, we will become new creations. God's going to weed that garden. But we are still uniquely us. And when it comes to the person God created you to be—your interests and your talents—God doesn't want you to change a thing; He wants you to grow close to Him and then use what makes you unique to make Him known to the folks around you.

Sure, God does plant us in places and situations where we may feel uncomfortable at times—places where we will be most dependent on Him. But we are also created to plant seeds in the circles in which we live and travel. That even includes our struggles. Hurting people can benefit from hearing how you deal with the challenges you face.

And when it comes to unique interests, just look at how my love of horses and farm life has enabled me to plant seeds in the hearts of other people who have similar interests, or maybe even folks who have similar struggles.

Others might find a place to plant a seed in the heart of someone who agrees with my dad, that horses are nothing more than "hay burners." Maybe you like cars or collecting Pokémon cards or you are a talented painter. When it comes to naming all the ways God made us unique and ways we are similar, the possibilities are endless. God loves variety, and as we plant seeds and patiently watch them take root, we will witness the colorful variety of souls blooming like the flowers in Kim's garden.

....

Lord, help me to be patient today as I plant seeds of faith and touch the lives of those in my care. Help me to learn from You—the patient Gardener. Help me to take to heart what Scripture says: "See how the farmer waits for the land to yield its valuable crop, patiently waiting for the autumn and spring rains. You too, be patient and stand firm, because the Lord's coming is near." Enable me to seek Your perfect timing. Amen.

8

PEAK EXHILARATION

The time is coming
when the people of Judah
will sing this song:
"Our city is protected.
The LORD is our fortress,
and he gives us victory.
Open the city gates
for a law-abiding nation
that is faithful to God.
The LORD gives perfect peace
to those whose faith is firm.
So always trust the LORD
because he is forever
our mighty rock.
ISAIAH 26:1–4 CEV

*T*odd swallowed hard as he faced his mountain. Today it was McKinley—the highest point in North America. Yesterday it was learning to live with a disability. If he reached the summit of the peak, he'd rank among the few elite climbers who have conquered this giant. Even more impressive, he'd have done it on a prosthetic leg—making him a conqueror of an even bigger mountain.

After resting at the top of a ridge, Todd continued his ascent up an extremely icy slope called Pig Hill. Everything he'd heard about the killer climb reinforced his fears—crevasses, glaciers, sheer ice walls, violent storms, plummeting temperatures, whiteouts. But this slope would determine his fate, pushing him beyond anything he'd imagined during his months of intense training. This wicked wall threatened to break him.

The rest is easy, he told himself silently. *Get past Pig Hill. The rest is easy.* But with each step a fresh spasm of pain exploded in his boot and seared the end of his stump. This was the most grueling climb of all, and it was taking its toll on his body. His lungs threatened to burst with every breath. His heartbeat drummed against his temples to the rhythm of his pain.

Just when he was at the point of giving up, his climbing partner pointed. "There it is—the summit!"

Todd gazed in awe. The summit seemed unconquerable. *We still have to go that much farther?*

But from Pig Hill it was an easy trek. Whether it was the gradual ascent or the adrenaline subduing his excitement, Todd maintained a slow but steady pace along the ridge at twenty thousand feet. Up ahead, another climber raised his hands in triumph. He had reached the summit.

Todd accelerated his pace and lunged the last few feet. His eyes caught sight of several flags left by previous expeditions. "Thank God!"

WISDOM FROM THE HORSE FARM

The Holy Spirit comforts us with perfect peace from God.

he shouted, and his voice filled every crevasse and canyon in Denali National Park.

After the McKinley expedition, Todd explained to a reporter, "I see myself as a representative of the 43 million Americans who, on any given day, are struggling against a major illness, a disability, or any other health-related challenge." He went on to describe challenges that wouldn't show up on any doctor's X-ray—divorce, death of a loved one, or overcoming drug and alcohol addiction.[3]

Here are two key questions every Christ-follower should come to grips with:

- What would happen if we stopped spending so much energy on our wants and needs or on the fear of our own shortcomings, and began to see the world—even ourselves—from God's perspective?
- What could the Lord accomplish through us if we would only get out of the way . . . and let Him have *His* way?"

In Todd's younger years—long before he even considered becoming a professional climber—questions about God and about his relationship with Jesus swirled around his head. But one day, while sitting in a park beneath a tree, he opened his Bible and began reading the Psalms. Then, he struggled to his feet and looked up through the branches and leaves into the sky. "Lord, I'm Yours," he prayed aloud. "Have *Your* way!"

After that everything changed for him. It was as if the whole world had opened up to him—adventures he'd never thought possible.

"I had climbed my mountains and seen the other side," he explained. "I had dodged thunderstorms, battled blizzards, endured incredible pain, and faced my fears through faith in God. I had gained a deeper experience with Him. Time after time, when it seemed the expedition was doomed, He smoothed the way. Time after time, when my body hurt so badly that I thought I couldn't take another step, He infused me with the strength to continue. Time after time, He was there. Now I know He always will be."

I talk a lot about the trauma that horses can carry; unfortunately, those are the stories that most people can relate to.

Like our horses, we have to work at overcoming our circumstances: we battle our sin nature, we forgive, and we learn to trust again. The list of all the things that we humans can struggle against is a long one. The same can be said about the lives of horses. You wouldn't think that there are actually horses that have had an Ozzie and Harriet kind of upbringing.

Years ago, I made the decision to take in a pregnant Norwegian Fjord Horse named Lovisa. Looking back, I admit this was a lot to take on at the time. But her circumstances tugged on my heartstrings, so I consciously chose to not overthink the situation and to make room in my barn for her and her impending bundle of joy. And of course, the financial side was the idea that I was getting "two for the price of one." *Sweet!*

I anticipated the birth of Lovisa's foal for months, and finally, one cool April morning in 2016, baby boy Oaken was born on our farm. He was, as my veterinarian put it, "the cutest baby I have ever seen." Oaken was covered in cream-colored fluff with a lighter cream-colored curly mane and tail. He looked just like a stuffed animal, and he was loved.

I will be the first to admit that when it comes to training foals, I'm pretty much clueless. Sure, they are born here at our farm all the time, but by the time they are old enough to be worked with, they are shipped over to my friend's barn. Thankfully, I am smart enough to at least admit my shortcomings, and I asked for help. Over the course of the few years I owned Oaken, he was handled daily and trained by some of the best. My seemingly "free" horse quickly became one of the most expensive in my herd—I ended up spending more in training than I received back when I sold him.

Oaken was covered in cream-colored fluff with a lighter cream-colored curly mane and tail. He looked just like a stuffed animal.

I loved Oaken so much that instead of investing in him for financial gain, I instead invested in giving him a great future by having him trained not to fear things.

In fact, to this day, I can't find one single thing that Oaken is afraid of. Leaf blowers, nope. ATVs, dogs, gunshots, *nada*! Oaken is not burdened by any cares.

Whatever he is presented with, no matter how scary it may seem, he just stands there stoically, as if to say, "You've never hurt me before, so I know that I am safe."

How many of us can be as confident as Oaken?

When I gave my life to following Christ, I was so relieved (and free) when I finally blurted out, much like Todd, "My life is Yours, Lord. I don't want it anymore!" It was the moment in which things were so out of my control I no longer felt safe. Up until that point it did seem as though I was in charge, orchestrating a pretty great future. But it was all an illusion.

God owns us, and He purchased us at an astonishing price.

We all know that salvation is freely given to those of us who accept it and repent of our old selves, but Jesus paid for our "free" gift by spilling His precious blood.

So why would we ever get the idea that God will not care for us when we are facing a mountain? Unlike Oaken, none of us can say that we have lived a burden-free life. But we can have Oaken's confidence because God has promised us that He has prepared a special place for us at the end of it all.

We can stand stoic believing that. No matter what comes our way, He always keeps us safe. Our Father's grace is not cheap. His precious blood showed us how much He invested in our future.

....

Lord, I know that You are my fortress, giving me victory over my sin and struggles. I need Your strength right now—Your perfect peace. Enable me to stand firm as I face challenges today. Help me to always trust in You because You are forever my mighty rock. Amen.

9

THE DAUNTLESS GALLOP

Do you not know?
Have you not heard?
The LORD is the everlasting God,
the Creator of the ends of the earth.
He will not grow tired or weary,
and his understanding no one can fathom.
He gives strength to the weary
and increases the power of the weak.
Even youths grow tired and weary,
and young men stumble and fall;
but those who hope in the LORD
will renew their strength.
They will soar on wings like eagles;
they will run and not grow weary,
they will walk and not be faint.
ISAIAH 40:28–31

I t's time to rock 'n' roll," Captain Charlie said to a pilot-in-training. The pressure hit as the F/A-18 Hornet Navy fighter jet descended to 500 feet above the earth, accelerated to 480 knots (530 miles per hour), and skimmed the ragged contour of the harsh desert below.

Charlie's mission: to coach a Navy trainee through some tricky low-level maneuvers.

The landscape became a reddish blur as Charlie's twenty-eight-ton Hornet picked up speed. He navigated his craft through canyons and over hills—sometimes sideways, sometimes upside-down. Just when his trainee didn't know which way was up or down, Charlie turned over the controls.

"No matter what conditions we face," he told his trainee, "always trust the instruments. Understand?"

"Roger, sir," the young pilot responded.

The trainee examined the instruments, then squinted out the window. The readings just didn't feel right to him.

"Rocks ahead," shouted the captain. "Roll right. Unload." (Meaning, "You're going to slam into a wall! Pull up and head out of the canyon.") After a couple of seconds of fumbling around, the trainee was still confused—and the plane continued on a collision course with a canyon wall. Suddenly, Charlie took over. The veteran pilot aggressively rolled the jet on its side and spiraled out of the saddleback, soaring high over a jagged ridge.

Once the plane had ascended to a safe height, the captain debriefed his student pilot. "You didn't listen to me," he stressed. "I'll say it again: *Never* go with your feelings in the air. Always trust the instruments."

"Yes, sir," the trainee said. "It's just that—"

"No excuses," Charlie barked. "The instruments will keep you on track. Now, let's go in and do it again."

The trainee swallowed hard. "This time, I'll do it right. This time, I'll trust the instruments."

As Charlie's flight trainees discovered, often the moments in life that truly mold our character are those filled with embarrassing flops and fumbles, not shining triumphs. And the key to surviving them—and eventually to getting back on our feet—is to trust your instruments. In the case of the believer, that means trusting in God's Word.

Christ-followers can experience a dauntless gallop in their faith if they are able to break free from doubt and take God at His Word. Have faith. Not only will He comfort us and help us through the humiliation of defeat, but He'll actually turn our sorrow into joy. In fact, He promises that we will "soar on wings like eagles."

It worked for Charlie, and I've seen it on the farm too.

Recently, I watched a video in which a cowboy got off his horse to tag a newborn calf—and the horse ended up protecting him from being charged by an aggressive mother cow. Whenever that cow got too close or attempted to charge the cowboy, his horse kicked.

To my amazement the cowboy never looked up once to see where the cow was. He just trusted the training he had invested in his horse.

Okay, a little bit of honesty here: If I were in that cowboy's boots, I don't think I would have the same level of confidence. I couldn't help but look up. My focus would be on that cow.

I've been hit by a mother cow before, and I'm sure that cowboy has taken that same beating a time or two. That he could turn his back on the cow is a testament to the trust he had in his horse to defend him.

On our farm we never had a horse that was that well trained, so we had to get creative. My dad wasn't a horse trainer or even a horse appreciator, but what he lacked in horse whispering he made up for in engineering. I swear he could weld paper if he desired to.

Dad was always devising plans to battle mother cows during calving

WISDOM FROM THE HORSE FARM

The Holy Spirit transforms flawed humans into heroes who are fit to accomplish His purpose.

season, kind of a comical battle. His first engineering attempt was a big red wagon that we would pull behind an ATV. We would lift the calf into this open-air wagon, and (in theory) the cow wouldn't try to follow. We'd be safe in the wagon—or so we thought. Until a cow jumped in with us one afternoon and flipped the wagon over. The calf, my dad, and the tagging box all landed on top of me. When I finally had the courage to uncover my head and look up, all I could see was my bow-legged dad running after the cow and calf.

This would seem discouraging to some, but then, you don't know my dad. With every blow from a mother cow, he got wiser, eventually creating what was affectionally known on our farm as the "Cowmmando."

The Cowmmando was an old blue Ford Ranger pickup that my dad welded into something that looked straight out of the 1980s movie *Mad Max*. To describe it accurately is impossible, but I will tell you that it was pure genius. First, you'd pull up next to the newborn calf and tug on a rope from the driver's seat that would open a door on the side of the truck. You would then climb down the stairs (yes, I said stairs), and then you could hoist the newborn calf into the covered bed of the truck so you could tag, weigh, and vaccinate without worrying about getting the smackdown from a panicked mother cow.

As crazy as it sounds, it worked! The Cowmmando was a creation that only time and experience could manifest. And it was inside the belly of this beast where I felt its safety. We had so much faith in that old truck that we could confidently turn our backs on the raging mother cows outside.

It was years later, after my dad sold all his cows, that he sold the Cowmmando to a rancher in Iowa. I sometimes wonder if it's still operational. One thing I can be confident in, though, is that no mother cow ever figured out how to penetrate its force field.

> The Cowmmando was a creation that only time and experience could manifest.

It's easy to have faith in an old truck when you watch your dad build it himself and you're able to test its strength in the field. But how do you find faith in someone or something that is not tangible?

It took some time and blows to fully understand that I can choose to believe that God tells the truth—or I can call Him a liar. I've wrestled with God. I've had lots of questions for Him to answer. And although I know He's not obligated to explain Himself, He's given me peace with most of it. He's revealed His character to me through Scripture, and I am confident that this world is not my end and that God loves me so very much.

We can't purchase that kind of faith, and it can't be given to us by family or friends. According to Romans 12:3, it is God who distributes faith to us. We don't deserve it, and we can't earn it.

God gives faith to His children, but then He gives us even more: instruments to help us strengthen our faith and to subsequently test it in the field.

Believing anything contrary to what the Bible says is a lack of trust in, to repeat Captain Charlie, "your instruments."

If I choose to believe that God doesn't care about me or my situation, I will feel unloved. If I believe that a circumstance will never get better, I will lose hope. Harking back to my experience with Dad's Cowmmando, make a choice not to focus on the cow.

From experience, I can tell you that when you don't trust the Word of God, you will never have enough confidence to turn your back on the chaos and sin of the world.

When I don't know which way is up or down, my daily Bible reading pulls me out of my slump. It's all part of God's training process. God provides times of trial and testing to prove that our faith is real and to sharpen and strengthen it.

We can all agree that this is not the same world we grew up in. But instead of focusing on all the bad in it, I choose to believe what my instruments tell me: that no matter what conditions we face, our future has never been brighter.

....

Lord, help me to soar—especially after moments filled with stinging flops and failures. Please give me a positive mindset and a heart that's faithful to You, regardless of my circumstances. Help me to trust the promise of Isaiah 40:31: "Those who hope in the LORD will renew their strength. They will soar on wings like eagles; they will run and not grow weary, they will walk and not be faint." Amen.

10

WORRIED TO DEATH

Let the peace of Christ rule in your hearts, since as members
of one body you were called to peace. And be thankful.
Let the message of Christ dwell among you richly as you
teach and admonish one another with all wisdom through
psalms, hymns, and songs from the Spirit, singing to God
with gratitude in your hearts. And whatever you do,
whether in word or deed, do it all in the name of the Lord
Jesus, giving thanks to God the Father through him.

COLOSSIANS 3:15–17

One minute Michael was laughing and enjoying "boys' night" with his son; the next he was pressing a cell phone tightly to his ear, motioning for quiet and fighting back tears.

"I don't think I'm going to make it," whispered a raspy voice on the other end. "I've been in and out of the emergency room all week. This time they had to drain fluids out of my chest. I'm back home now, propped up on the couch. Tired. Just sitting here, waiting . . ."

It was his older brother Jerry. His voice was hoarse, his words labored. He was medicated again—heavily drugged.

Jerry had cancer.

He'd been battling it for nearly two years—twenty-four hellish months of blood tests, MRIs, CT scans, PET scans, simple X-rays, physical therapies. Poking. Probing. Jabbing. Injecting. There were constant visits with chemical oncologists, radiologists, pulmonologists, countless surgical procedures and thousands and thousands of dollars spent on drugs—some that appeared to do more harm than good, others that promised to be the silver bullet against cancer. Yet despite an all-out medical assault, Michael's once-robust brother was steadily withering away—turning into a listless, emaciated patient, a victim of a terminal illness.

Michael had to accept what he'd tried hard to deny: Jerry was dying.

"I'm so sorry," Michael said slowly and deliberately into the phone. The pizza parlor was loud and his connection was weak. "I'm so very sorry. I think you can beat this. You've fought so hard."

"I'm tired, Mike . . . very tired." Jerry paused, then spoke again, a bit more reflective. "I've tried to do some good in this life, to help people, to be there for them—"

"Yes, you have. You've been there for me."

"I don't think I'm going to make it."

"I'll keep praying."

"Pray. Yes—please do. And know that I love you. That's why I called. I just wanted to tell you that."

"I love you too."

"I've got to hang up now . . . got to go."

"Goodbye, Jerry."

"Goodbye."

As Jerry's name faded from the screen, Michael stared at his phone in disbelief. *Is that it? Are those the last words I'll ever say to him?*

He looked up and scanned the restaurant. So many smiling faces—couples and families, first dates and retirees. Just to his right, two middle-aged men in ties were swilling beers and talking business. A grandmother was doting on a toddler to his left. Directly in front of him, a young man and woman were celebrating. *An anniversary? A pregnancy? A first home?*

Everyone all around him was laughing, toasting, talking . . . *living.*

And then his gaze landed on his son. Christopher had that deer-in-the-headlights look in his eyes. "Daddy, you're sad," his ten-year-old said. "Is everything okay?"

Michael forced a grin. "Yes. Things will be all right. Uncle Jerry is really sick today."

"He's always sick." Christopher picked up a slice of pepperoni and held it awkwardly. "Is he . . . you know . . ."

"It's hard, but let's talk to Jesus about him. God knows just what to do."

"Okay, Daddy—okay."

I'd guess you could say that Michael is my "calming goat," and if you're not familiar with that term, it's a goat that is paired up with a skittish racehorse to keep it calm.

As Michael sat in the restaurant, sorting through all the raw emotions inside, he began to see clearly how fear had become his own cancer—spiritual stumbling blocks that were robbing his relationships with God and with his family. In a very real sense, he was allowing Jerry to slip away, even before he was gone—allowing himself to die, even before his life was over.

Anxiety, worry, and fear were robbing Michael of *life.*

In fact, Michael traced it all the way back to his early childhood—right around the time he was just six, when his father abandoned his family. And the cycle grew as he watched his mom worry her way through what must have felt like an impossible job: she had to raise six kids all by herself! Michael was the youngest and certainly the most high-maintenance of her children.

"Mrs. Ross, that boy of yours is such a worrywart," his first-grade teacher once told her during parent-teacher conferences. Then she grabbed his mom's hand. "Is everything okay at home? How are you holding up?"

Michael held his breath, selfishly worried that his mom would say something that would make his family—actually, *him*—seem different . . . inferior. *Will my teacher stop liking us? Will the other kids think we're weird?* (As an adult, he has cut himself some slack. After all, first graders aren't supposed to worry; they're *supposed* to have a childhood. Sadly, Michael didn't.)

Junior high was a nightmare. "Come on. Don't be so scared of the ball," barked Mr. Battle, Michael's PE instructor. (Yep—his name was actually *Battle*, which ironically described the hell Michael endured day after day.) "Man up. Put some muscle into it." During moments like that, Michael would have given anything to melt into the cracks on the gym floor. *Sorry, Mr. Battle, but I don't exactly feel much like a man. Most of the time, I just feel scared.*

College was better. "This boy can write," one of his professors said of him in front of a classroom filled with his peers. And then read something aloud that Michael had written. It was his first journalism assignment, and his professor was a hard-nosed newsman who seemed otherwise impossible to please. The affirmation built Michael up—until negative self-talk and the anxiety-fear-worry cycle brought him down again. *But what kind of a future will I have? The competition is fierce among writers. And don't most of them starve?*

Marriage changed everything. "You know it's all going to be okay," Michael's wife, Tiffany, often tells him. "God's in control. Do you actually believe this? All the worry in the world isn't going to change a thing. It won't bring us more money or make us more acceptable . . . or cure a terminal illness. Can you take a faith step and trust God with the things that worry you? Can you trust Him enough to release all these fear traps?"

Praise God for godly women! Praise God for life-mates we can lean on, lovers who gently nudge us back to the cross. *She really knows me—the person I am inside, worry warts and all—yet she loves me anyway,* Michael often reminded himself. *I don't have to perform or mask my flaws. I am acceptable just as I am.*

Just a few days after Father's Day, Michael's cell phone rang, and Jerry's name flashed on the screen. Michael paused for a moment, savoring each letter of his name. And then he pressed "accept." But before he could say hello—

"Michael," a voice interrupted, "it's your brother." Oh, that raspy voice that Michael loved so much. It was still labored but a little less medicated. He continued: "I just wanted to wish you a late happy Father's Day."

A big smile stretched across Michael's face. Imagine that: his brother was terribly sick, yet he had called him. He wasn't giving up, but instead he was *living* . . . celebrating every precious, God-given breath he'd been given.

WISDOM
FROM THE
HORSE FARM

The Holy Spirit helps us break
free from fear and worry.

"Happy Father's Day to you, my brother," Michael said to him. "Has your son been over to see you?"

"Oh, all the time. He's been so good to me!"

"I wish I could be there with you. I wish we didn't have three states between us."

"It's all good, Mike . . . it's all good. Give Tiffany and Christopher a hug. And give yourself one too. I love you, brother."

"I love you too."

"Goodbye for now."

If only the kind of fear Michael struggled with were the amusement park variety. You know—the type that merely plays with adrenaline, tickling our senses shortly after we buckle ourselves into a car on a roller coaster. We're usually pretty confident that nothing worse than losing our lunch is going to happen. And we're at least somewhat certain that the ride will be over in thirty seconds, gently delivering us to that long line we waited in for thirty minutes . . . just to get scared! Amusement park fear is a mere imitation of real, raw fear.

The types of emotions Michael has dealt with all these years relate to apprehension, worry, stress, and anxiety. They can range in severity from mere twinges of uneasiness to full-blown panic attacks marked by rapid heartbeat, trembling, sweating, queasiness, and terror.

I can relate because I've been there too.

Sometimes these feelings are connected to everyday worries and strike out of the blue. Other times they are a bit more out of proportion, even unrealistic—and are triggered by specific struggles. For example,

the abandonment Michael experienced as a child makes him especially sensitive to issues of death and loss. So, watching his brother endure a terminal illness was horribly painful for him. Michael loved his brother. He didn't want him to suffer, and he certainly didn't want to lose him. But Jerry lost his battle with cancer not long ago.

While death and loss are major stressors for everyone, they are intensified in the lives of those who battle anxiety. Yet God is teaching Michael to surrender anxiety, worry, and fear—and He is replacing them with faith. That's what God is teaching me too.

I have known Michael (or "Mikey," as I call him) for a few years now. He is the other writer on this book and all my other books before this one. To say that God gave him talent for writing is to understate the gift. He's incredible.

In fact, I've made it pretty clear to anyone in the publishing world that if Mikey isn't going to be involved with me in the writing process, then I'm just going to stop answering my phone—which is my standard response to my insecurity. If I have a choice between fight or flight, I almost always pick flight.

I'd guess you could say that Michael is my "calming goat," and if you're not familiar with that term, it's a goat that is paired up with a skittish racehorse to keep it calm.

How funny is it that our heavenly Father provided me with someone whose biggest challenge is anxiety, and God is using him to calm *me* down! There's no pun involved, but I'd say that's a pretty great dad joke.

During the COVID-19 pandemic—when we were not allowed to meet

I'd guess you could say that Michael is my "calming goat," and if you're not familiar with that term, it's a goat that is paired up with a skittish racehorse to keep it calm.

in small groups at church—my friend Ashley and I decided we'd make our own small group of two. Ashley is another person in my life who struggles with bouts of overwhelming anxiety—the unproductive crippling kind. On one particularly hard morning for her, the Enemy had even convinced her that she didn't "have enough faith to be saved."

Michael's story reminded both of us amid the pandemic that fear was robbing us of life. Satan had gotten his foot in the door by stealing our peace, so much so that we realized we weren't living in the moment or feeling very hopeful for the future. Instead, we were in panic mode, trying to prepare for some bad thing to happen.

I had to ask myself, *What does it say to my heavenly Father when He has provided me with so many blessings this week, yet He doesn't even get to see me excited by His gifts?*

Our small group made the choice one morning to make some life decisions that didn't include our standard, "what if" backup plan.

We decided to bask in the peace we had been given today.

How about you? Are you able to let God's provision be a daily reminder that He loves you? He will always take care of His children regardless of the circumstance. We don't have to be worried to death. We can live as if our future has never been brighter. That's always been our Father's plan.

....

Lord, I want the peace of Christ to rule in my heart. Drive out fear, and show me how to live in peace. Give me a thankful heart, and let the message of Christ dwell in me. Amen.

PART 3

God's Spirit Makes Us Kind and Good

11

BUCKED OFF MY HIGH HORSE

Submit yourselves, then, to God. Resist the devil, and he
will flee from you. Come near to God and he will come
near to you. Wash your hands, you sinners, and purify
your hearts, you double-minded. Grieve, mourn and wail.
Change your laughter to mourning and your joy to gloom.
Humble yourselves before the Lord, and he will lift you up.
JAMES 4:7–10

It was a raw, rare "oh-crud" moment for Philip. One second, the camp director was riding confidently atop Spur, a handsome mustang who stood fifteen hands high. The experienced horseman was demonstrating basic riding techniques to a group of enthusiastic junior high horse lovers. The crowd's oohs and aahs felt pretty good. *They're lovin' this,* Philip thought to himself, *and I'm totally on my game today!*

But without warning, a series of loud, startling sounds—*SMACK!*
THUD! CRUNCH!—sent Spur into crazy-horse meltdown . . . and ended up launching Philip high into the air. Nearby ranch hands had dropped a crate they were unloading from a truck, and that had spooked the horse.

With his arms flailing and his body rocketing above the arena, everything seemed to slow down, at least for a split second. Just below him Philip could make out the wide eyes of his slightly amused, slightly traumatized

WISDOM
FROM THE
HORSE FARM

The Holy Spirit replaces
pride with kindness.

kids . . . the mouthing of unrepeatable words from his staff . . . the violent bucking of his crazed mustang. And then came the inevitable: a loud *thud* as his body made contact with the ground.

"Ouch," he whimpered.

Philip slowly sat up and ran through a quick, mental self-triage: *No blood. Everything is still attached. No harm done! (Just a seriously bruised ego.)*

"My horse freaked, which is completely out of character," Philip later explained to his campers. "He bucked me off for the first time ever."

And since Spur is big and strong, Philip said the buck felt like a bomb had gone off under his backside. It was a sharp vertical acceleration—like nothing he had ever experienced before. But when he came back to his senses, the words of James 4:10 raced through his brain: "Humble yourselves before the Lord, and he will lift you up."

The greatness of God should humble us. Yet for most people being humble brings to mind a form of weakness. As believers we must walk in the footsteps of our Lord and place ourselves under His loving guidance. As we walk in humility, we enjoy the day-to-day release from stress, as God intended. Not so with pride.

The Bible has some tough words about pride: "Pride goes before destruction, a haughty spirit before a fall" (Proverbs 16:18). We all need to be bucked off our high horses from time to time so we can fall on our knees before Jesus.

Sure, I've been bucked off my horse more times than I care to remember, but I'll never forget how it stings when I've been bucked off my high horse.

These have been moments when my cringeworthy comeuppance has been put on display for all to see. Around six years ago I had the wild idea that I wanted to homeschool my kids, yet because—as I have been reminded on numerous occasions—I'm not exactly qualified, and I've got my hands full looking after farm critters, I decided to take a different approach. I got together with some other parents with the same desire, and we found a way to pool our resources. What's more, we hired two teachers who actually knew what they were doing.

Our modernized one-room schoolhouse was born, we were an official homeschool "group," and it was good. Well, at least for a while.

Kids were everywhere on my farm, reading to God's creation outside, catching frogs for science, and taking regular trips to the fishing hole. We were living my homeschool dream. It was *Little House on the Prairie* but with internet.

Then some real drama unfolded in our community, and it wasn't the lighthearted, Walnut Grove kind that you'd expect from Harriet Oleson.

One of our teachers was having a hard time keeping up with the number of kids in our group. The differing ages and abilities seemed to overwhelm her. And by giving 100 percent of herself to each individual

student, she was quickly burning out. On top of that, I will admit, I was not giving her my full support. You see, I was unwilling to do the job myself, but willing to spout off about how easy it was to do.

"Just put some papers in front of them and let them get to work," I'd tell her. "This isn't that difficult."

You see why I need Jesus?

The short version of this is, thankfully, this teacher humbly stuck it out despite my behavior. But teacher number two did not.

And this is where I had to eat a heaping portion of humble pie.

Wow! You teachers! I praise you, because for the rest of our school year, my friend Tracy and I filled in the gaps that teacher two left behind. We were exhausted by the end of it all. We saw—and experienced—what the other teacher was trying to tell us the whole time. Teaching is difficult; I know that now.

Humility means we put others above ourselves, and it's painful when the Holy Spirit lets us know when we are being cocky and proud because usually it ends with us being put to the ground. In this case He fed me dirt.

Jesus values humility.

> We were living my homeschool dream. It was *Little House on The Prairie* but with internet.

....

Lord, the Bible tells me that striving to be humble is serious business to You, so I want it to be serious business in my life too. I want to submit myself to You and Your will. Give me the strength to resist the devil, and draw me into a closer walk with You. Clean me up, purify my heart, and help me to be humble before You. Amen.

12

UNWRAPPING HOPE

You have dealt well with your servant,
O LORD, according to your word.
Teach me good judgment and knowledge,
for I believe in your commandments.
Before I was humbled I went astray,
but now I keep your word.
You are good and do good;
teach me your statutes.

PSALM 119:65–68 NRSV

I t was Christmas Eve—a joyful time, a family time. So why did David feel so depressed? For one thing, he and his mom were alone.

David was seventeen, and his five older siblings (three brothers and two sisters) were grown up and out of the house—and unable to come home for the holidays. As for his father, he had deserted the family when David was a young boy.

The truth is, his dad was an alcoholic—and his mom would never allow alcohol in their house. So, about the time David was learning to ride a bike, his mom was forced to take a tough love approach: "Get help, and learn to be a proper husband and a father," she had told David's father, "or follow your addiction—and lose your family. You can't have both."

David's father chose his addiction. It was a decision that broke their hearts and cracked the foundation of his family. Yet in the years that followed, his mother was determined to mend some of the fractures and to hold their family together. Amazingly, she succeeded. (To this day he and his siblings share a deep bond that was nurtured by their mother.)

But on this particular Christmas, David didn't feel very festive. He missed the chaotic, Grand Central Station atmosphere that usually filled his house.

"Yep, this is going to be a sorry holiday," he mumbled to himself as he slouched down in a recliner and stared glumly at his Christmas tree.

Does this thing actually have branches? he wondered. Their tree was covered with so many ornaments and candy canes and strands of popcorn that it was nearly impossible to see anything remotely spruce-like.

David squinted, noticing a brightly colored decoration that he had made years earlier—and then a few that his sisters had created. *Mom saved them all,* he thought. *This tree is like a time line of our lives.*

As he followed the time line, memories flooded his mind. Mostly good ones.

David's eyes focused on an oddly shaped antique bulb passed down from his grandmother. He couldn't help thinking about all the family traditions his mom had established. She was so proud of their heritage, which could be traced back to England, Ireland, and Sweden.

David spotted a furry, hand-stitched reindeer his mom had made—which triggered images of the long hours she'd worked cooking, cleaning, and doing everything possible to keep a roof over their heads.

> Their tree was covered with so many ornaments and candy canes and strands of popcorn that it was nearly impossible to see anything remotely spruce-like.

Suddenly, his thoughts were interrupted by the sweet smell of chocolate—then a warm smile.

"Let's open a gift," David's mom said, handing him a cup of cocoa. "We always open one present on Christmas Eve—and this year shouldn't be any different." Before he had a chance to utter a word, she plopped a big package on his lap.

"No, Mom, let's just forget about it," David protested. "Everything's all wrong this year."

His mom lifted an eyebrow. "I'd say things are pretty right," she replied.

David shook his head and groaned. His mom continued.

"Look around you," she said. "Look at where you live, and consider the food you get to eat. Some people in the world don't have any of these things. And think about the people who love you—like your brothers and sisters. They may not be here physically, but we're still a family. A strong family."

Secretly, David was tracking with everything his mom had to say, but his teenage pride wouldn't allow him to admit it. Instead, he glanced at the package on his lap and gently tugged at the ribbon. When the last piece of wrapping paper fell to the floor, the gift was revealed.

He looked up and gasped. "Mom! You can't afford this!"

"I'm the gift giver here . . . so I'll decide what I can and can't afford."

David's mom had practically emptied her savings account on a present that he had talked endlessly about for years yet had always thought was out of reach. She had bought him a 35-millimeter camera, along with various lenses.

"Every young journalist should learn to use a camera, right?" his mom asked.

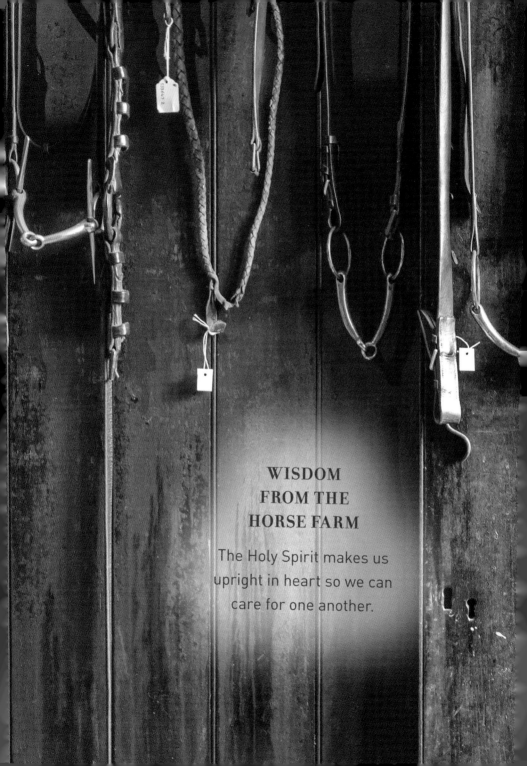

WISDOM FROM THE HORSE FARM

The Holy Spirit makes us upright in heart so we can care for one another.

David sat speechless, feeling as if he were holding not just a camera but some sort of link to his future. "This is amazing!" he said as he fiddled with the gadgets.

"There's a carrying bag in the box too," his mom said. "I figure you can take this to college with you next year."

A grin stretched across David's face. "Mom, *you're* pretty amazing. You sacrifice so much for us. What would we do without you? Who would we be?"

Suddenly, Christmas didn't seem so empty. What's more, David saw his mom differently. For the first time in his life, he truly respected the incredible woman God had created her to be. And from that moment on, his world made a lot more sense.

That night, David unwrapped the greatest gift a teen could ever receive. It wasn't just an expensive camera that had caught his attention. David's mom had given him something far more valuable: *hope.*

And it was her goodness through God that opened the door.

Despite the hardships in David's life, his mom sacrificed so much for her children, planting seeds of faith in their lives and sparking hope for the future.

The Bible says that goodness in action reflects God's kindness and goodness toward us. The Lord shared His kindness and goodness through salvation (Titus 3:4) and continues to "show the immeasurable riches of his grace in kindness toward us" for all eternity (Ephesians 2:7 NRSV).

I'll never forget a moment when my own children unwrapped hope. It was the day our Shetland pony, Tucker, came to our farm. Dan

and I decided to surprise our kids with him, so we tied him near their playground. When my son and daughter came home from school that afternoon, we handed them a treasure map that led to a little black bundle of joy grazing next to their swing. It was a special moment for us.

A few years later, my kids outgrew Tucker's size, so an old cowboy friend told me I should sell Tucker. Actually, his exact words were, "He's a worthless eater."

My heart was heavy, but I thought it was probably the most logical choice. After all, because he was so small, he wasn't any good to us anymore. I prayed and pondered the situation. Looking back on that moment of stress, I can't believe I even considered getting rid of Tucker.

One day, over social media, my cousin shared a story about her daughter, Aila. She reminded me of what a difference even the least of us can make in this world when we choose to reflect the light of Jesus with a thankful attitude.

Aila had found a tiny mirror and was showing it to her mother. "It's so little," her mom pointed out. "What are you going to do with it?"

Aila responded, "Well, Mom . . . it can still reflect!"

Nothing can convict you more than a hopeful kid who refuses to see the negative in a situation. Aila chose only to see what she could do with the small blessing she had been given.

Instead of focusing on the problem, that Tucker was too small, I started focusing on the things I really loved about him. His patience and his gentle demeanor were such blessings, I wondered what I could do with them. *I know*, I thought. *I can share what makes him so special with other people.*

I have taken Tucker to visit kids at schools, and he's really popular when I take him to visit the residents at the retirement home.

I also invite kids and parents over to our farm to paint Tucker's hooves with glitter paint. Sometimes I even dress him up in funny costumes. Tucker has been the Grinch at Christmas, Pegasus, a pirate, and a firefighter. But my favorite costume was created by a group of kids who dressed him up as Maximus Decimus Meridius, the main character in the movie *Gladiator*, played by Russell Crowe.

I invite kids and parents over to our farm to paint Tucker's hooves with glitter paint. Sometimes I even dress him up in funny costumes.

Tucker is a little guy who makes a big impression wherever he goes. He's been a great evangelism tool I can use to reflect the Savior I serve. I am so thankful I am able to share him with other people.

David's mom changed his perspective when she dared to point out all that they had to be thankful for. His little Christmas turned out to be pretty great when he realized how his mom used those small blessings not for herself but to reflect the love of Jesus into the lives of other people.

Yes, thank God for what you have but also for what you are able to give. As long as there is love in action, there will be hope.

....

Lord, I want to keep Your Word in my heart. And as You are good and do good, I want to go and do likewise. Let me share Your love and kindness with family, friends, and strangers. Let me always point others to the hope we have in You. Amen.

13

WHEN A HATFIELD FORGIVES A MCCOY

Don't make God's Spirit sad. The Spirit makes you
sure that someday you will be free from your sins.
Stop being bitter and angry and mad at others.
Don't yell at one another or curse each other or ever
be rude. Instead, be kind and merciful, and forgive
others, just as God forgave you because of Christ.
EPHESIANS 4:30–32 CEV

Forgiveness. Oh, how Kelly longed to experience it. Yet her family didn't quite understand what it meant to forgive someone, and they even prided themselves on being distant relatives of the Hatfields, who—according to legend—had a long-standing feud with a Kentucky family known as the McCoys.

Kelly's childhood had been marred by abuse. Parents who abused alcohol—and her. Dark closets. Nightmares and family secrets.

One evening during church service, Kelly, by now a young adult, realized that Jesus had died for her and decided it was time to receive Him in her heart. She wanted God to be her Father. In fact, Kelly wanted everything her church family had talked about: eternal life, forgiveness, love.

If the purpose of her past was to bring her to this moment in time, Kelly felt it was worth what she had gone through. So, she prayed and wept tears of repentance. Jesus was now real to her. She felt the love of the Father pouring down on her. Kelly's cell group wrapped their arms of love around her and praised God for the miracle in her life.

Fast-forward five years: Kelly married the love of her life, a young man named Jeff, and she has grown in God's knowledge and grace. However, even though she and Jeff have a supportive fellowship family, Kelly's relationship with her parents is completely broken. In fact, she does her best not to think about her past.

In the months that followed their marriage, Jeff and Kelly became avid hikers.[4] During one of their treks on property Jeff had inherited, they discovered a piece of paradise in the woods—and even began making plans to build a log cabin at the location.

The view was spectacular! Sunsets blazed magenta and scarlet. Deer fed in the valley below. The blue, misty mountains of West Virginia rolled across the horizon.

Over the next few months, Jeff and Kelly drew sketches and discussed how they could build the cabin by themselves. Then the two hiked to the site, hammered wooden stakes into the ground, and attached string to form the layout of the cabin. They planned to have an expansive front porch that overlooked the Blue Ridge Mountains.

Eager to get started, Jeff and Kelly broke ground, slinging shovels full of dirt into a wheelbarrow. Then, suddenly, they encountered a problem. Jeff hit something solid with his shovel. It just wouldn't budge.

In the exact place the foundation footers were to be dug, they discovered a root of massive proportions beneath the surface. Swinging the mattock as hard as he could and striking the root with all his might, Jeff couldn't even chip it. The thing seemed to be petrified.

As Kelly watched her husband battle the root, a wave of emotion overtook her. She sat on the ground and continued to watch. Jeff attacked the root from every angle—then discovered that the main root had a network of smaller roots that were intertwined and gnarled together underground. This is what made the ground rock-solid. Frustrated, Kelly got up and walked away. She simply couldn't give up their plans to build the cabin on this spot with the perfect view. After hiking to a rock cliff high above the valley, she pulled out a pocket Bible and began to read.

Quietly, God spoke to her: "*The root is deep and it has become hard like stone. Even though it is deep and seems impossible to remove, it isn't. You can't remove it alone, but I will remove it for you if you will allow Me to.*"

It was a moment Kelly would never forget. She felt the awe of God speaking intimately to her. And she knew that her Father wasn't talking about the root Jeff was trying to remove. He was referring to the petrified root in her heart. She had tried to keep the hate and lack of forgiveness hidden below the surface. Now she wanted them out of her life.

Right there on that ridge, the love of God began to melt her—and tears fell. Squeezing her eyes shut, she prayed, "I can't deal with this any longer, Lord. Remove this lifelong root of pain and bitterness. Take it away from me, and in its place give me love and forgiveness. Heal me from my past. Let me love the family who hurt me. Allow them to see Your love living in me, and save them in Jesus' name."

The sun can melt butter, and it can harden clay. Those substances have no say in how they react to the sun's powerful rays.

WISDOM FROM THE HORSE FARM

The Holy Spirit helps us to forgive one another.

But we have a choice in how our hearts react when exposed to the Son of Man. We can choose to harden our hearts, like the petrified root Kelly talks about, or we can choose to follow Jesus and let Him soften it.

Kelly's story is a powerful one. It teaches us that anything is possible with Jesus. Those bitter roots can grow so deep into our hearts, and some of our bitterness can even be justified. People hurt people all the time, and emotional scars can be far worse than even a physical fracture, which can be placed in a cast and mended. Sometimes it's just easier to walk away or to compartmentalize our lives so we don't have to deal with the circumstances or interact in complicated relationships. We put our pain on a shelf and play the "forget about it" game. All the while we can't see that we are nurturing a spirit of bitterness that refuses reconciliation.

I'm a compartmentalizer myself, and although I talk about how forgiving horses are, they are also smart enough to be self-preserving. Fool them once, but watch how they won't be hurt again.

I've witnessed this in one of my own rescue horses. LuLu was sweet on the ground, but basically impossible to ride. One moment, I could be on her back, quietly making our way through a field, and the next, fear would harden her body. Suddenly, she would bolt, and the situation would get unsafe, not only for me, but for anyone in our proximity.

A horse trainer once told me that LuLu must have experienced something that terrified her so much that she'll never get over it. I appreciated the honest advice from the trainer, who then asked why I was wasting my time with her when I had safer horses back at the barn.

I decided to let LuLu live out her life in the pasture and free her from stress. She is now safe and happy there.

Sadly, I've seen horses worse off than LuLu. Some have been hurt so badly their defense is to lash out.

Thankfully, we are not horses, because who would want to live like that? Why do some of us choose such unbridled wrath? LuLu didn't have a choice, but we do.

We have Jesus.

By the time Jesus got to my heart, it was pretty cold. Soft enough to let Him in, but He definitely needed to pack a sweater. I can't count on my fingers how many relationships I just walked away from because I was able to.

Just like an outburst from my horse LuLu, my protective measure was to cut people loose before they got too close. I'm a runner. This kind of behavior would confuse people, and since bitterness is contagious, I'm sure that caused damage to them as well. The world is a cruel place, and I made sure I pointed that out to them.

> By the time Jesus got to my heart, it was pretty cold. Soft enough to let Him in, but He definitely needed to pack a sweater.

Many of us, even after we have given our lives to Jesus, still feel too cynical for Him to make clean. I have seen a lot of things and have been disappointed, but over time I became a new creation. Jesus gave me my sensitivity back.

When Jesus becomes our personal Lord and Savior, He starts a work in us. Over time, He will make us better. He will shine truth on our circumstances. He will bring better insight to our situations.

I realized what I was doing to myself by withholding forgiveness from others. I was expecting God to forgive me but not anyone who had hurt me. But the Holy Spirit gently pointed out, "Look at all the hurting you have created, and I've forgiven you." My bitterness was the by-product of unforgiveness. Yet my cool heart turned to putty in *His* hands.

Christ forgives as we forgive others. Take a good hard look at Matthew 6:14–15. There, Jesus tells us that our Father will not forgive our sins if we don't forgive those who sin against us. Our Savior's words in these verses are tough—and may even make your knees weak. Search your heart: As in Kelly's life, is there any darkness or resentment that you'll be held accountable for? As you search your heart, keep this in mind: God's nature is forgiveness. (Check out Exodus 34:6–7.) He wants to work forgiveness into our hearts.

The Lord worked deep in Kelly's heart that day on the cliff. And by the love and grace of a mighty God, she is being healed and made whole. Today, both roots—the one in her heart and the one on her land—have been removed. The cabin is complete and sits in the perfect place, with spectacular views. And after years of silence, Kelly and her family are talking again. In fact, her family even visited her and Jeff. As Kelly and her family sat on her big front porch—the one that overlooks the blue, misty mountains—she was amazed. *The view seems so much better now,* she told herself.

Lord, I, too, desperately want forgiveness in my life from friends, family, neighbors . . . and especially from You. And I want to forgive others. I want to stop being bitter and angry and mad inside. I want to be kind and merciful and to forgive others, just as You have forgiven me. Teach me to forgive. Amen.

14

GETTING THE UPPER HOOF

Shun youthful passions and pursue righteousness,
faith, love, and peace, along with those who call on
the Lord from a pure heart. Have nothing to do with
stupid and senseless controversies; you know that they
breed quarrels. And the Lord's servant must not be
quarrelsome but kindly to everyone, an apt teacher,
patient, correcting opponents with gentleness. God may
perhaps grant that they will repent and come to know
the truth, and that they may escape from the snare of the
devil, having been held captive by him to do his will.

2 TIMOTHY 2:22–26 NRSV

When Lynn's husband, Bob, set out to bathe their first broodmare, a dark brown beauty named Sugar, he had no idea the challenge he faced. After four years of racking up championships across the county, Sugar knew more about wash racks than Bob did. And Sugar had an attitude.

The horse planted her hooves five feet from the broad concrete slab. Bob tried to pull her, coax her, and pick at her, but she wouldn't move. Lynn could see that Sugar was cool, calm, and self-centered, reminding her of a Hollywood starlet yawning while examining her manicure.

"What's wrong with this stubborn horse?" Bob shouted in desperation. "I can't get her to budge."

Why did Sugar refuse? Because she could. A big grin stretched across Lynn's face. "You're right," she said with a chuckle. "Sugar isn't going anywhere with you. That's because she's being a pig." (*Pig* is the equestrian term for diva.)

Frustrated, Bob handed Lynn the lead rope. After the experienced horse trainer had a little talk with Sugar—brushing her and telling her what she thought of her horse's behavior—Sugar sweetly walked into the wash rack while Lynn's husband fumed behind them.

Lynn pointed out that horses give us the gift of simplicity—seeing the world through their eyes. "There is no pretense with these animals," she explained to Bob. "They're direct and only say what they mean."

Horses also give us insight into ourselves—our own strengths and weaknesses, she told him. "Folks often assume that the horse is at fault when it fails to learn a lesson. It's more likely that the horse either didn't know what to do, or it didn't trust you . . . or maybe it simply beat you at your own game."

And that day, Sugar got the upper hoof![5]

WISDOM
FROM THE
HORSE FARM

The Holy Spirit enables
us to avoid quarreling
with each other.

Staring down fifteen hundred pounds of stubborn horse can teach us how to learn faith and focus. Horses are as simple and silly as three-year-old children but as wise as Yoda. They help us carry the weight of worthy leadership. Horses also help us understand that limited commitment always produces limited results and that love is the most powerful motivator.

Lynn's thirty years as a horse trainer, most of them working with stallions, taught her to be simple and direct and to own every word, action, and breath. In her years as a Christian, she's learned that God lightens burdens, speaks into our needs, holds us, shakes us, teaches us, and sends us.

Step-by-step, lesson by lesson, the Holy Spirit helps us become more like Jesus:

> The Lord's servant must not be quarrelsome but kind to everyone, able to teach, patiently enduring evil, correcting his opponents with gentleness. God may perhaps grant them repentance leading to a knowledge of the truth, and they may come to their senses and escape from the snare of the devil, after being captured by him to do his will. (2 Timothy 2:24–26 ESV)

Each of us has been called to serve, to make disciples the same way Jesus did. No matter our audience, flock, or herd, our job is guiding others to a relationship with Jesus—and ultimately to transformative faith. And there are so many ways we can do this. For me it's natural to use stories from the horse farm as a way to talk about Jesus.

The fact is, I'm a pony person. Either you are or you aren't. It's as simple as that.

I have heard my whole life how "mean" Shetland ponies are in particular, and I'll admit I've seen scars and I've heard battle stories of all the times ponies have cut loose on kids: running them into fences, bucking them off in the dirt, and biting them in the seat. The idea is that if they can make the kid afraid of them, then they'll be put out to pasture and never have to work. Ponies are stinkers, but they are also thinkers.

So be still my beating heart! I *love* ponies! Especially my Shetland pony, Tucker. Just writing his name makes my heart brim over with all the feels.

I purchased Tucker years ago. I had originally bought him for my kids, and because I know that Shetland ponies do have a reputation for being a handful, I made sure Tucker was vetted for anything that would be problematic.

Be still my beating heart! I *love* ponies!

I used Tucker as a way to train my kids on how to behave around horses. I had sought out a pony whose reaction to their mistakes wasn't to kick or to bite. He did let Reagan slide off his back a few times and into the dirt. That's where his forty-inch stature is ideal.

Ponies aren't completely different from full-size horses; they're just better gifted at honing in on our weaknesses and then using them to their advantage—which also makes Shetland ponies extremely comical and so very charming.

Tucker has been known to flip manure carts, steal tools right out of tool belts, and run away with manure forks. He took full advantage of my old barnyard helper Lindsay. Except when I was also present; then Tucker was a perfect gentleman.

Lindsay was always curious as to why that was. I would say, "Tucker knows who butters his bread, Lindsay." Also, as long as you allow Tucker to get away with these kinds of hijinks, he will always have the upper hand.

Unfortunately, sometimes Satan also can get the upper hand on us no matter how schooled we are in Scripture, because we are weak in the flesh.

As much as we accuse Shetland ponies of being troublemakers, humans are also a handful! All Satan has ever done is observe the weakness of man and make ways for us to fail miserably. He gets in our heads, and suddenly we believe we lack the tools necessary to be useful to God. Satan steals from us, he flips our hope on its head, and he trips us up as we run. Not charming! We respond by either lashing out in fear or refusing to move at all.

But Jesus will never put us out to pasture and leave us there. He won't take us out of this race because of our inabilities or weakness.

The Holy Spirit is direct with us; He corrects us, then uses our mistakes to His advantage.

Jesus keeps it simple: He tells us only to "follow" Him. If we are willing to do that without ceasing, our weakness will reveal His glory to those who are watching in a way that's almost charming.

Lord, Your Word today instructs me to not be quarrelsome but kindly to everyone. Show me how to do this, and redirect my steps when I'm in danger of veering off Your path. Show me how to set the example for younger believers—ever patient, correcting opponents with gentleness. Give me opportunities to make disciples. Amen.

PART 4

God's Spirit Makes Us Faithful

15

BORROWED-TIME BELIEVER

Come now, you who say, "Today or tomorrow we will go
to such and such a town and spend a year there, doing
business and making money." Yet you do not even know
what tomorrow will bring. What is your life? For you are
a mist that appears for a little while and then vanishes.
Instead you ought to say, "If the Lord wishes, we will live
and do this or that." As it is, you boast in your arrogance;
all such boasting is evil. Anyone, then, who knows the
right thing to do and fails to do it, commits sin.
JAMES 4:13–17 NRSV

The plane is down . . . with no survivors? An act of terrorism! Steve frantically scrolled through flight information on his computer, desperately trying to make sense of the chaos unfolding around him. Suddenly, five ominous words jumped off the screen: *Flight 11 . . . Sequence Failed Continuity*. (Pilot-speak meaning the plane never reached its destination.) Across the room his TV replayed horrific images of a smoking hole in the World Trade Center—right along with the title "Flight 11 Hits the North Tower."

Steve turned to his wife and wrapped his arms around her. "That's the trip I packed for," he said, his voice cracking and his entire body trembling. "I should have been on that flight, yet for reasons only God knows, my life was spared!"

It was Tuesday, September 11, 2001, and nineteen al-Qaeda terrorists had hijacked four passenger airliners midflight. Two of the planes, American Airlines Flight 11 and United Airlines Flight 175, crashed into the north and south towers of the World Trade Center in lower Manhattan. Steve, a full-time commercial airline pilot and a part-time church planter in rural Maine, was scheduled to command flight 11. Yet a simple computer glitch had bumped him off the flight—essentially sparing his life.

In the days and weeks that followed, God would show him what it means to live like a "borrowed-time believer."

Steve opened his Bible to Hebrews 11:1–3 and read: "Now faith is the assurance of things hoped for, the conviction of things not seen. Indeed, by faith our ancestors received approval. By faith we understand that the worlds were prepared by the word of God, so that what is seen was made from things that are not visible" (NRSV).

"Life is but a blink of an eye," Steve told his wife, squeezing her hand. "So, I'm doing my best to savor life—knowing that every day, every moment, every breath is a gift from God."

Christ-followers grow their faith by putting their trust and confidence in the stable footing of Jesus Christ. If we trust Jesus as our Lord and Savior, then we have confidence that we'll spend eternity with Him. And that makes a difference in how we live each day.

That's how it was for Steve. God used the events of 9/11 to change him from a man contentedly doing His will as a pilot in a small town in Maine

WISDOM
FROM THE
HORSE FARM

The Holy Spirit gives us
the faith to believe.

to a man consumed by the urgency of reaching a nation for Christ. Romans 8:28 tells us that God works all things together for His good. In the years following September 11, God has shown Steve what that good looks like.

The Lord has done the same thing for my family.

Regardless of how long life may seem to be, it's a flash in the pan compared to eternity. We should live like it. But I have to be transparent with you: I don't always live this way. At least, not *all* the time.

I'm so glad when Jesus was asked to bear the burden for my sin, He didn't reply with, "I can't," or "I don't want to get involved," or "Maybe some other time."

I wonder sometimes if I am putting too much focus on storing what I perceive as essential items down here. Steve's account is sobering to the fact that something as mundane as a computer glitch could end his time on earth, or not. Steve definitely was awakened to the sense that each day, minute, second of time allowed on earth is only time borrowed from the One who created it for him.

Here's one thing I've learned about a reborn life of following Jesus: knowing what is the right thing to do yet sitting idle is actually a sin in itself. As Steve shows us, we are *all* borrowed-time believers. We need to live today with an eternal focus because, as Scripture challenges us, "What is your life? For you are a mist that appears for a little while and then vanishes."

....

Lord, I put my faith and trust in You. I, too, am a borrowed-time believer. I am thankful that You have given me eternal life and that all my tomorrows are in Your hands. Strengthen my faith. Help me to savor every moment and to do what is right in Your eyes. Amen.

16

BACK IN THE SADDLE

For surely I know the plans I have for you, says the Lord,
plans for your welfare and not for harm, to give you a future
with hope. Then when you call upon me and come and
pray to me, I will hear you. When you search for me, you
will find me; if you seek me with all your heart, I will let
you find me, says the Lord, and I will restore your fortunes
and gather you from all the nations and all the places
where I have driven you, says the Lord, and I will bring
you back to the place from which I sent you into exile.

JEREMIAH 29:11–14 NRSV

It wasn't the sport of barrel racing that left eighteen-year-old Amberley paralyzed from the waist down. Her life was forever altered by something far more mundane: a routine drive along a stretch of Utah road she'd been on a million times.

As the rodeo star headed home from a competition, she rounded a bend and spotted something blocking the road. Amberley slammed on her brakes and swerved to miss the object—she thought it was a crate or a piece of furniture. As she twisted the wheel, she overcorrected, and her truck rolled. Tragically, Amberley was ejected from her seat.

Several days later she woke up in an intensive-care unit with her mother's warm smile staring down at her. Soon, the smiles turned to harsh reality. Once Amberley had grown stronger, doctors had to share her difficult prognosis: "You'll never walk again."

Tears rolled down Amberley's face. *Never walk?! That means never ride.* She suddenly felt as if all her dreams had vanished right before her eyes. Amberley looked up at her mom and uttered two words she thought she'd never say: "Sell them."

"Just sell all my horses," she continued. "I won't be able to care for them . . . or ever ride again."

A stern expression washed over her mother's face. "Nope—that's not going to happen," she said matter-of-factly. And then she reached over and took her daughter's hand. "Do you remember the times when your horses had been injured? You waited for them to heal. So, this time, they will wait for you."

Her mother was right. Eighteen months later, Amberley was back into competitive barrel racing! Her hope returned—right along with her competitive nature. "She's like any other rider when she's on a horse," Amberley's mom told a friend. "She gets to leave the wheelchair behind, and the horse becomes her legs."

And six years after that, Amberley is consistently winning competitions again. Here's what she posted on her Facebook page:

> I am so excited I might have cried. This is the FIRST buckle I have won since my paralyzing car accident six years ago! To make it even more special, I won the 1D on my little horse Legacy, which is the first horse I've trained without my legs! This just made me realize that even though I'm strapped to my saddle, even though I can't kick, even though I am in a wheelchair I can still train a barrel horse![6]

WISDOM
FROM THE
HORSE FARM

The Holy Spirit draws
our hearts to God.

A tragedy turned to victory. This young competitor is closer to Jesus Christ now than ever.

"My faith in God has grown," Amberley told a group of students at a nearby church. (In addition to barrel racing and being a breakaway roper, she serves as a motivational speaker.) "I needed to depend on Him for strength when times were the hardest or even when I still have days of challenges. I know that I wouldn't be where I am without my family, friends, and my Lord and Savior."

Before the trauma Amberley said her relationship with God was "on the back burner" in her life. "While I was a believer, my faith wasn't as strong as it could have been," she says. "In my life, rodeo was the first thing I thought of when I woke up and the last thing when I went to bed. I couldn't imagine life without it, and I never thought I would ever have to."

She was even featured on the *Today* show, telling the host, "Ever since I was three, my happiest place on earth was sitting on my horse's back. Now that happy place has greater meaning as I draw closer to the One who has given me life. Through Jesus, my goals are very focused: walk, ride, rodeo!"

The hardest thing for nonbelievers to wrap their heads around is how we believers can still praise God when tragedy happens. Tornadoes, barn fires, physical struggles . . . it's a never-ending list. God can get us out of each of these things at any time, so why do we still trust Him when He chooses not to? What good can come out of tragedy?

My horse Sven cut his leg on a jagged fence board a few years ago. The wound was deep enough that it required treatment, and since it was the middle of summer, it needed to be kept dust- and insect-free. So, I decided to separate him from his buddies in the field and move him into

the barn. Believe me when I tell you, I had to hear about it. He made sure to let the neighbors and me know how unhappy he was. You could hear his megaphoned cries from inside the barn. But as the hours passed, his cries came further apart. He accepted his circumstance and began to even appreciate that he was not contending with the biting flies in the field. He certainly loved the extra attention and the barn fan.

That night a fierce storm (maybe even a small tornado) came up unexpectedly. The winds were strong enough to pull a gate off its hinges and also flip a heavy hay feeder over a fence. The feeder was then tossed through the pasture where Sven would have been standing. I couldn't help but think what a blessing it was that Sven had cut his leg instead of getting hit by that hay feeder.

Moments like these make you wonder how God uses what seems to us like a bad thing to orchestrate our lives through this fallen world. God is all-knowing, omnipresent, and all-powerful. Because we don't share those qualities with God, we can never understand all that He is up to.

Like Sven in the barn, when tragedy strikes, we cry out, and we're not happy about our circumstances. But we also know that God hears us, and He cares deeply. He tends to our wounds. We grow closer to Him because He has our attention, and we grow deeper in love with Him, which reflects outwardly to others.

God's desire is that all people will spend an eternity with Him. Sometimes to get us there He needs to get our attention, and we see His blessings even when things are hard. In Amberley's story, He got her attention and used her circumstance to bring her into a closer relationship with Him, and she now lives a life that reflects His love.

She is an amazing witness.

Lord, I call upon You and am praying with all my heart. I want to know You better and to be close to You. I want to know the plans You have for my life. Hear my prayers. With each step I take, I'm searching for You, and I'm seeking You with all my heart. Amen.

17

WARM BREAD FOR THE SOUL

Though you have not seen him, you love him; and
even though you do not see him now, you believe
in him and are filled with an inexpressible and
glorious joy, for you are receiving the end result
of your faith, the salvation of your souls.

1 PETER 1:8–9

Early each morning, even before the rooster crows and the sun peeks over the Blue Ridge Mountains, Frieda goes to work at her tiny West Virginia bakery. It's just a stone's throw from the town of Beckley, and it's a hit with locals. People line up outside her door every day except Sundays to buy her warm buttered bread.

Frieda and her family hand-mix eggs, oil, flour, yeast, and milk in large bowls. Then a whole bunch of other ingredients—such as honey, cheese, oats, sun-dried tomatoes, and flaxseed—are added to the bowls of dough to make an assortment of mouthwatering breads. The family recipes, passed down for generations, are seemingly endless.

Sticky lumps of dough are turned out on floured wooden boards and are kneaded and dropped in greased pans. As the dough gently rises, overflowing the sides of the pans, a glaze of beaten egg whites is lightly brushed over each loaf. Then comes the final step: the pans are placed in hot brick ovens and baked until the bread turns a perfect golden brown.

Can you smell the aroma? The heavenly scent of hot baking bread drifts through the streets outside the bakery—and no one can resist it! People line up outside the shop, and Frieda gets busy bagging the baked loaves and adding a note to each one: "With love from my family to yours. 'For by grace you have been saved through faith. And this is not your own doing; it is the gift of God'" (Ephesians 2:8 ESV).

Still wearing her bakery apron dusted with flour, Frieda offers customers samples of her delectable creations, and she makes recommendations on which loaf goes well with a specific meal. People bring their selections to the counter, some purchasing bread to share with coworkers for lunch, others requesting that their loaves be wrapped up in brown paper for dinner. Everyone leaves the store smiling and toting trophies in paper sacks.

Regular customers know there is no need to buy more than they can use in a day, because every morning there will be more wonderful, aromatic, fresh bread baking in the bakery's oven. Frieda's family tradition of baking bread has continued faithfully every day for the past fifty years.

The experienced baker points to the Lord's promise in John 6:35: "I am the bread of life. Whoever comes to me will never be hungry, and whoever believes in me will never be thirsty" (NRSV).[7]

Like Frieda's customers, when we smell the wonderful, glorious aroma of the Bread of Life, we hunger for it. We must have it! When we taste it, we want more. This bread fully sustains us. This Bread is life and health and peace.

Our heavenly Father knows what we need even before we ask. Before the sun rose this morning over my Nebraska farm, before I crawled out of bed and prayed my first prayer, He understood my needs and desires.

**WISDOM
FROM THE
HORSE FARM**

The Holy Spirit fills us
with joy as we put
our faith in God.

He heard the deepest unspoken cries of my heart. My Lord knows I need His daily bread to make it through the day.

My neighbor Brenda jokingly says that if there were such a thing as reincarnation, she would want to come back as one of my horses.

My horse farm is more of a horse Hilton: heated stalls in the winter, fans on in the summer, special areas with padded flooring, pastures full of green grass up to their hocks. Yep . . . I agree with Brenda: my farm is ridiculously cozy, and my critters live carefree and comfortable lives.

That's probably why almost weekly someone asks me if I would like to take their horse off their hands. I get it; people have kind hearts, and sometimes they buy a hard-luck case at a sale barn, or they just don't have the time for their animals anymore. Sometimes it's the money required to keep them up. People are sweet enough to try to find good homes for their horses to move into. But as I get older, I am becoming more and more allergic to horses. So, my days of taking in more horses are unfortunately over. I am content with the number of horses I currently own, even though I feel forced into limiting the number.

The most important lesson that was revealed to me during the whole COVID-19 ordeal is how much of that year I spent trying to orchestrate my own comfort. I live a life much like my horses. I have more than I need. I'm living the padded-flooring, heated-stall lifestyle that supersedes the basic necessities of life, such as food, water, and shelter. Here in the United States, most of us live this way.

I guess I am at least proud of the fact that I was never the person buying shopping-cart loads of toilet paper, but I'm not proud of the fact that even though I had more than enough, I wasn't willing to "spare a square."

I blew so much of my testimony just hunkering down and not helping to meet the needs of others. Being "comfortable" is an idle setting for me, and it keeps me from experiencing the things that I also need spiritually.

So, what am I saying? I'm not saying to go out and give it all away. But I have spent the remainder of my time shedding excess stuff and finding contentment with what I have. I have also just flat out stopped trying to orchestrate comfort in my kids' lives. How hard do we try to keep our kids out of situations that may make them feel uncomfortable?

> Being "comfortable" is an idle setting for me, and it keeps me from experiencing the things that I also need spiritually.

Coping with discomfort is a great lesson to teach our kids. It's what will give them the courage to try new things and meet new people. It forces them to be dependent on God for the things they need today. Harder for me is not praying to God to help them find good jobs or surround them with good friends but praying, "Whatever it takes to get them to You, Lord." Now, that makes me uncomfortable!

The most important thing we need for ourselves, our kids, our friends, and our families is to find our own personal, dependent relationships with Jesus. Sometimes that means working our way through, or watching others work through, hard and uncomfortable circumstances. Like me, trying to orchestrate my own comfort, only to discover that all of the "extra" comforts weren't going to sustain me.

I could hoard all the bread, but the excess will just turn moldy before I can gobble it up. That doesn't do anybody any good. The excess is worthless.

What I love so much about Frieda's story is that the warmth that flows out the door of her bakery every day is met with the people in the community taking for themselves only what they need for that day.

What a hard but powerful lesson to master. We must run toward heaven and ask Jesus only for enough of what is required to take the next step.

....

Lord, thank You for being the Bread of Life. Thank You for never leaving me hungry or thirsty. Even though I have not seen You with my own eyes, I know You and I love You. I believe in You, and as Scripture says, I am "filled with an inexpressible and glorious joy." I am "receiving the end result of [my] faith, the salvation of [my soul]." Amen.

18

COAL MINER'S DAUGHTER

Do not store up for yourselves treasures on earth,
where moth and rust consume and where thieves break
in and steal; but store up for yourselves treasures in
heaven, where neither moth nor rust consumes and
where thieves do not break in and steal. For where
your treasure is, there your heart will be also.
MATTHEW 6:19–21 NRSV

Tiffany struggled to keep from falling as she hiked up a muddy West Virginia holler. It was a typical February day: gray sky, frigid temperatures, and melting snow that turned the ground into mud. Cold air stung Tiffany's face and hands, and her boots were slipping and sliding as she walked along the wet dirt road.

"How much farther?" Tiffany yelled to her dad. He was a few steps in front of her.

"Almost there," Floyd hollered back. "Come on, kid!"

Tiffany paused for a moment and looked around. Suddenly she realized that she had been in this place many times before. The frozen landscape made it look more like a trek through Siberia than the backroads of Pineville, West Virginia.

"Dad, a lot of people live in this holler," Tiffany said. "It's going to take us hours! Are we really visiting them all?"

Floyd gave a thumbs-up. "Yep. That's why we've got to keep moving."

It was Saturday morning, and Tiffany was helping her dad with his church bus route. In typical West Virginia style, the community they visited was tucked up in the mountains, which made it impossible to reach without four-wheel drive. So, they parked his big red Oldsmobile just off a main road and hiked to each house to invite the residents to church.

After what felt like their hundredth visit, Tiffany couldn't help but notice that her dad had a way of making everyone feel special.

Floyd was a coal miner, so these were his people. He always knew some personal detail about a family's life, something that drew them into a conversation. And as the two walked from house to house, Floyd filled Tiffany in on each backstory, giving her tips on what to say and what to steer clear of.

Suddenly a familiar voice interrupted their conversation. "Floyd and Tiffany! Well, aren't you a sight for sore eyes!"

Tiffany looked up and saw a skinny, unshaven man in worn-out flannel. He waved and flashed a warm smile.

"Hello!" Floyd fired back.

After sharing a hot pot of soup with the family in the two-room house, they walked back outside.

The father looked back toward the house, as if ensuring that his family couldn't hear him, then said, "Floyd, I need a word with you."

"I was laid off three weeks ago and can't find another job," he continued, shamefaced. "I can't bear to tell my wife, so for three weeks I've been leaving the house to look for a job. But my wife and family think I'm going to work every day. I don't know how I'm going to break the news to them. I just need a job."

The conversation tugged at Tiffany's young heart. Here was a good man who was in a tough spot. He wanted to work. He wanted to take care of his family, and he was so embarrassed that he was no longer able to provide. His wife was probably used to him bringing home groceries every week, so she would surely know something was wrong in a couple of days when he came home empty-handed.

After a long pause, Tiffany's father offered the man some encouragement: "I'm going to help you out. You're a good man and a good worker. We'll find you some work."

A smile stretched across the man's face as he let out a sigh of relief. Floyd asked the man to come see him in town the next day, and he would give him some job leads. He also told him that he could list him as a reference. "One last thing," Floyd said. "I'm going to load you up with some groceries from the church's food bank." He would put them in grocery bags so it would look like the man had just come from the store.

As Tiffany and her dad walked back to the car that morning, Tiffany wasn't worried about her boots getting muddy or how cold the air was. She was more interested in why her dad would disguise the groceries so the man's wife wouldn't know they were free. "Isn't that deceitful?" she asked.

Her father grinned and said, "Sometimes it's important to give a man a little dignity."

Tiffany learned so much walking around in those mountains with her father during her childhood. As her dad modeled how to treat people with dignity and respect, she learned the importance of consistency and generosity. She learned how to take care of people. She learned the skill of seeing the world from someone else's point of view. But most of all, she learned how to love people the way Christ loves them.

Tiffany would give anything to walk around those muddy hollers with her dad again.

If you drive through the tiny West Virginia coal mining town of Pineville, you won't see billboards with photos of a man named Floyd plastered on them, and you won't see statues erected in his honor. But if you mention his name, you'll bring smiles to a lot of people's faces—especially from his daughter Tiffany. "I am a coal miner's daughter and proud of it," she says without hesitation. "But I'm most thankful to be the daughter of a man who taught me to follow Jesus."

On the farm, horses bind our hearts and feed our souls. And like a warm blanket of affection that drives away the cold, a horse hug gives us the assurance that we are loved. Unlike people, horses don't expect us to "fix" ourselves, in all our fallenness, before accepting us. We don't have to fix our weaknesses before we can be acceptable to God either. He loves us just the way we are. And like a soothing horse hug, the faithful promises of God are hugs from heaven, and the Bible is full of them.

When I purchased my first horse, Orlando, as an adult, he came with a saddle and a whole lot of promises. I promised his previous owner that I would never sell him. I also made a commitment to Orlando—that I would always choose what was best for him no matter how inevitably hard I knew some of those horse decisions could be.

I purchased Orlando back in 2013, and he was already a geriatric by definition. At the time, I was dealing with some painful digestive issues, so his friendship was a great distraction from my agony. He was in my life when I made the decision to follow Jesus, and Orlando is the cover model on my first book, *Unbridled Faith*.

In 2020 Orlando turned twenty-four, and I decided I would retire him. He had been out at my friend's barn, connecting with teenage girls at the time. This was a gift he had—not a gift unique to horses, but Orlando did seem to have a little extra something special when it came to making a broken girl feel whole again.

The second day of Orlando's retirement at my farm he aspirated some grain, and although I called the vet right away, his old grandpa lungs could not take the stress of it all. He contracted a terrible case of pneumonia in both lungs, and the vet nudged me toward putting him down. I countered with a secondary option of draining the fluid off of his lungs and giving him twenty-four hours to make an underdog turnaround. Although this plan gave my O-man a small amount of temporary relief, his lungs inevitably filled back up and I instructed the vet to do what I knew was right.

I let him go.

Seeing our commitments through is not always easy. In fact, I think when you have a commitment to someone or something, you should probably expect things to be harder.

I don't know if you feel the same way, but horses in general are easier for me to be committed to than people; people come with conditions. But when we commit to following Jesus, we are also committed to loving His people even when we encounter difficulty.

> I think when you have a commitment to someone or something, you should probably expect things to be harder.

Tiffany's dad, Floyd, saw past the human condition and instead stayed committed to always trying to do what is best for the folks in the holler, and he stayed committed

WISDOM FROM THE HORSE FARM

The Holy Spirit leads us to true, everlasting treasure.

to that all the way to the end of his race. I'm sure there were plenty of opportunities for Floyd to say, "Okay, God, they're Yours," and take his out. But then it would have sent the conflicting message to Tiffany that his commitment to Jesus ends when the holler gets muddy.

What we believe about our future determines how we live today. Most Christians who have made a mark on this world were not aiming for earth but for heaven.

Lord, Your Word says, "Where your treasure is, there your heart will be also." I want to store up treasures in heaven, and I want to be obedient to Your mission for my life. Help me to set my focus on You and to grow closer to You. Give me the courage to point everyone I can to the life I have found in Jesus Christ. Amen.

PART 5

God's Spirit Makes Us Gentle

19

HEAVENLY BUS ROUTE

But in your hearts revere Christ as Lord. Always be
prepared to give an answer to everyone who asks you to
give the reason for the hope that you have. But do this
with gentleness and respect, keeping a clear conscience,
so that those who speak maliciously against your good
behavior in Christ may be ashamed of their slander.

1 PETER 3:15–16

As Beamon sat on his front porch, sipping sweet tea and gazing at a star-filled Tennessee sky, he reached over and gently took his wife's hand. He felt as if he were sitting on top of the world—counting more blessings in his life than there were stars in the sky. Topping the list was his Lord and Savior. Years ago, Jesus had cleaned up his heart, replacing anger with gentleness, washing away his sins, and giving him a whole new life. Beamon was blessed with a faithful wife, who loved and cherished him, and he served an important role driving a tour bus for a popular entertainer. At times, his job entailed being more of a spiritual caretaker than a driver.

Beamon's mind flashed to countless "heavenly bus routes" he'd rumbled along through the years: sharing God's wisdom with the celebrity he served and witnessing to strangers in some of the cities they visited.

Beamon took another sip of tea and thought about when he had first become a Christ-follower. He remembered how excited he was and how he'd wanted to give 150 percent to serving Jesus. Yet he lived so hard for God that his intensity ended up driving people away.

"He's that weird religious guy," people would say behind his back. "Nicer than most . . . just a little too crazy for God."

A big grin stretched across Beamon's face as he reminisced with his wife. "You've been so patient with me . . . and I've come a long way, haven't I?"

His wife smiled back. "The Holy Spirit has grown you into a gentle servant," she said.

"I had to learn that I was saved by grace," he added. "And the best thing we can do with God's grace is share it with others."

That's exactly what this heavenly bus driver has set out to do.

> "I had to learn that I was saved by grace," he added. "And the best thing we can do with God's grace is share it with others."

By the grace of God, he was able to forgive his parents and let go of a painful past. (His childhood had been marred by brokenness and violence.) Beamon had even led his dad to the Lord just hours before his father passed away. And when Beamon and his wife had taken a big leap of faith—packed up the house they'd lived in for twenty-five years to start fresh in another town—God had given him a heart for his new community. A short time after settling in, Beamon led his eighty-three-year-old neighbor in a prayer of salvation . . . just a few months before his new friend died.

WISDOM FROM THE HORSE FARM

The Holy Spirit replaces anger and brashness with gentleness and grace.

That had sparked an urgency in Beamon's heavenly bus route. Giving 150 percent to serving Jesus is good . . . but letting His love flow through him was even better!

"And to think," Beamon told his wife, "I didn't grow up in a godly home. I didn't know anything about salvation or about Jesus. Yet the Lord got ahold of me and radically changed everything."

Admittedly, it had been a rocky road for several years. He was stalled in the same Sunday school class with the same teacher, learning how to be a godly man, a godly father, and a godly husband. "Eventually, the Lord knocked some sense into me," he said. "The Bible tells the story about a believer whose sins were many, yet she was forgiven. And so 'she loved much' [Luke 7:47]. I, too, have been greatly forgiven . . . and have come to love others very, *very* much."

Just like my friend Beamon, I, too, am learning a thing or two about grace. Here's a Bible truth that literally brings me to my knees: God is crazy in love with me!

He knows every detail about me because He knit me together in my mother's womb (Psalm 139:13). He is so meticulous about me that He has even counted how many hairs there are on my head (Matthew 10:30). And despite the dirt in my life, He chooses me. I'm worth it to Him. He would literally die for me . . . and He already has!

Know what? God is crazy in love with you too. As Christ-followers, you, Beamon, and I are victorious in Jesus, as you can see from this passage:

Then I heard a loud voice in heaven. It said,
"Now the salvation and the power and the kingdom of our God
     have come.
The authority of his Messiah has come.
Satan, who brings charges against our brothers
     and sisters,
has been thrown down.
He brings charges against them in front of our God day and
     night.
They had victory over him
by the blood the Lamb spilled for them.
They had victory over him
by speaking the truth about Jesus to others.
They were willing to risk their lives,
even if it led to death."

REVELATION 12:10–11 NIRV

Back in the height of my husband's comedy career, we were on the road more days than we were at home. In the entertainment business you keep striking that hot iron until the day your popularity grows cold. In this fickle world, fame is temporal, and you accept it.

So, for the first four years, we raised our kids while rolling down the road in a tour bus, and Beamon became the believer who greased the wheels of our spiritual lives. Ninety percent of the people who were with us on that tour bus are now in a relationship with Jesus. Part of the reason

is that Beamon's faith walk showed us that forgiveness and restoration take more than just imagination.

Just like long-distance running, forgiveness is a process. It doesn't just happen when you commit your life to following Jesus; it happens moving forward . . . step-by-step. When I first made that commitment myself and I was holding unforgiveness in my heart toward someone, I'd say, "Jesus says forgive, so I forgive this person." Done.

But after time, old thoughts would creep in, Satan would drudge up old wounds, and I was back to anger toward the people I claim to love. *I'm not much of a believer,* I would think. *Maybe I'm not even saved if I am still thinking this way about this person.*

I was still mistakenly believing that forgiveness is a feeling. But true forgiveness is a commitment to pardon the offender.

I know in my own life how many times I have sat idle, waiting for an apology that I was never going to get. I didn't realize that by standing idly in my spiritual life, my faith muscles were cooling down. Satan was getting a foothold on me in the form of resentment.

It wasn't until I realized the magnitude of the forgiveness Jesus had extended to me that I fully understood the need for me to forgive certain people in my life. If Jesus doesn't withhold His grace from me, I have no right to withhold my grace from other people. So, I began to pray like this: "Jesus, I am committed to forgiving this person despite how I feel, and I may have to keep doing it again and again all the way to the finish line."

I don't think there is anything that weakens the Enemy's power over us more than when we commit to forgive someone. That doesn't mean always inviting those who are forgiven back into our circle or accepting abuse. In other words, commitment does not always eliminate the consequences of their actions.

I love Beamon's story. He didn't just toss Satan off at the bus when he made the commitment to forgive. Beamon went beyond what the world's version of forgiveness is, and he prayed that his offenders would follow Jesus with him. That is forgiveness that we don't have to imagine, because we've seen Jesus do it Himself.

Lord, clothe me with compassion, kindness, humility, meekness, and patience. Help me to bear with others, sharing the hope I have in You. Let me always be prepared to witness to everyone I encounter. And enable me to speak with gentleness and respect. Amen.

20

HORSING AROUND
WARMS THE HEART

*"Come to me, all you who are weary and burdened, and I
will give you rest. Take my yoke upon you and learn from me,
for I am gentle and humble in heart, and you will find rest
for your souls. For my yoke is easy and my burden is light."*
MATTHEW 11:28–30

Dr. Lew approached his agitated Appaloosa with a familiar, "Hello, Bennie," and then began to gently brush the horse. "You're a beauty," he said with another stroke. "So, what got you spooked on the trail? You're home now . . . safe in your stall."

The horse's blanket of brown spots seemed to leap right off its stark-white coat. At first Bennie was twitchy and would try to pull away. But Dr. Lew's soothing, rhythmic brush strokes slowly built trust between human and horse. Gentleness was a favorite language he used with the animals on his Oklahoma ranch, a language he often used with people too. It was a healing solution. As a professional horse whisperer and an ordained minister, he had discovered that healing solutions in both vocations practically mirror each other. Dr. Lew helps troubled horses

by gently building trust with them and responding to their needs—two techniques that mend human relationships as well.

"There's nothing mystical about what I do," he says. "It all comes down to really good cause-and-effect training. I get to the heart of what's troubling man and beast, I figure out the best way to help, and then I set them on a healing path."

This seasoned rancher knows that horses simply cannot be fooled. They are great judges of a person's character and moods, so when we are feeling burdened, they sense our low energy and feel how we are feeling. Dr. Lew watches the horse's natural reactions as he tries to soothe the animal, and then he takes note of how the horse benefits and grows from his help. "Horses are insecure and defensive by nature," he says. "They respond very well when their caretakers understand their needs and take the steps to put them at ease. People aren't much different."

Back at his church—just a stone's throw from his ranch—Dr. Lew applied what he calls the "language of the horse" to the needs of those in his care: "Healthy relationships bring healing into our lives," he preached from the pulpit. "I've seen it with the horses on my ranch—especially an Appaloosa named Bennie. Whether we've grown up broken like Bennie and are having a hard time finding people we can really trust and learn from, I know Someone who will never let us down. He freely gives us the healing we desperately need."

The "whisperer minister" then opened his Bible and began reading Jesus' words in Matthew 11:28–30: "Come to me, all you that are weary and are carrying heavy burdens, and I will give you rest. Take my yoke upon you, and learn from me; for I am gentle and humble in heart, and you will find rest for your souls. For my yoke is easy, and my burden is light" (NRSV).

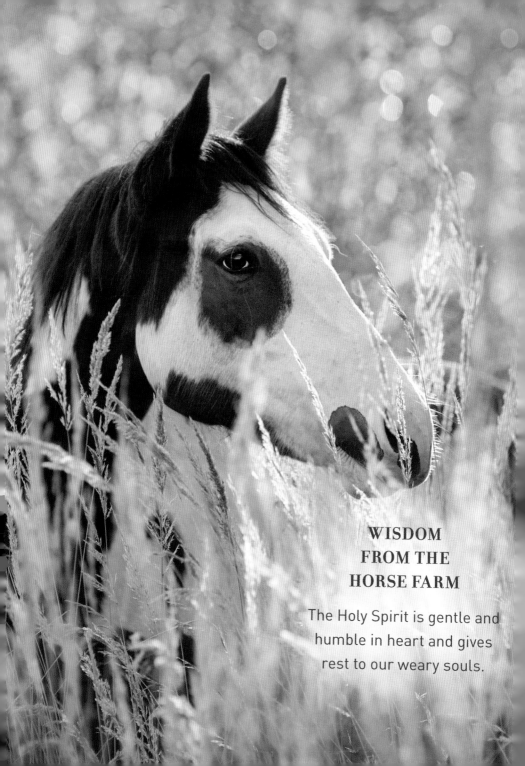

WISDOM
FROM THE
HORSE FARM

The Holy Spirit is gentle and
humble in heart and gives
rest to our weary souls.

Having a relationship with our Creator, not to mention the horses and the people we live with, begins with trust.

God designed us for relationships. Everything we do is built on the connections we share with those we love—whether they have four legs or two! And I've found that He brings horses into our lives when He knows we need them most—whether we are lonely or deep in grief. In moments of vulnerability, horses encourage us and build us up. I have a horse named Rethel who helped a teenage girl mend a heart bruised by mean boys and bad friends. A pony named Charlie Brown helped another young person's heart heal from bullying. Orlando, my first horse, whom I mentioned earlier, took my mind off some health struggles.

But no matter how amazing horses are, the ultimate healing comes only from the Father. God will bring the right scriptures, worship songs, and people into our lives when He knows we need them most. When we are lonely or in deep grief, He will send us His love in creative, diverse ways—through nature, an email, or a movie scene. As we learn to trust Him to comfort us, we learn to go to His side more and more.

When we feel injured and beaten down by circumstances, sin, and hurtful people, we can take our pain to God. He will mend our brokenness. In fact, Scripture tells us that the Lord will restore our joy: "You make known to me the path of life; you will fill me with joy in your presence, with eternal pleasures at your right hand" (Psalm 16:11).

Some things are beyond human repair and can be restored only by the loving kindness of the Savior. We can trust His healing work.

No doubt about it, 2020 was an interesting year to say the least. Not all bad, but there were definitely some challenges. During the height of all the crazy, our dog Berry became very ill.

I knew when I examined Berry's mouth and saw that his gums had gone pale that his situation was dire. I called the vet and got him in right away. But because it was during the height of the "Fifteen Days to Slow the Spread" campaign, "in" meant that I had to meet a vet tech in the parking lot of the vet office.

She took Berry into the clinic, and I waited in my car. About ten minutes later, my veterinarian came out to deliver the news that things weren't looking so great for my friend. I knew it, so no surprises there. But between the wait in the parking lot, the state of the world at the time, and now worrying about my ailing friend, to my surprise I was carrying more stress than I realized. Whether or not I was willing to admit it, my soul needed rest.

As I sat with my car door open, having just learned that Berry had a fifty-fifty chance of survival, my veterinarian, Dr. Brown, reached out his hand and patted me on the knee, saying, "I will do the best that I can."

Suddenly, I felt a sense of relief that I didn't even realize my soul was craving. It was the reassurance that spoke into my soul that everything would be okay no matter the outcome. I took a deep breath.

Just like Dr. Lew reassuring Bennie, Dr. Brown's human touch soothed my weary soul. Even though Berry didn't make it through his health crisis, I'll never forget Dr. Brown's caring words. As we run our

marathon toward heaven, we have to remember that our souls need to rest along the way. Too often we get busy, beaten down, spooked on the trail, or even burdened by the feeling of being stuck in the monotony of life. That's when we forget to renew and energize.

Jesus will give us rest. He has promised that things will be okay no matter what, and we are refreshed by that promise. And while we are resting, God is still working.

Lord, I often get weary and feel burdened by the trials of this world. Thank You for Your comfort. Thank You for giving me rest when I need it. As the Scripture instructs, I will take Your yoke upon me and learn from You. Thank You for being gentle and humble in heart and for giving me exactly what I need. Amen.

21

DIFFERENT, NOT DEFECTIVE

You are the one
who put me together
inside my mother's body,
and I praise you
because of
the wonderful way
you created me.
Everything you do is marvelous!
Of this I have no doubt.
Nothing about me
is hidden from you!
I was secretly woven together
deep in the earth below,
but with your own eyes
you saw
my body being formed.
Even before I was born,
you had written in your book
everything I would do.
PSALM 139:13–16 CEV

S ix-year-old Amy had known only two gazes during her young life: the warm, reassuring smiles of family and friends . . . and the cold stares of total strangers.

She and her mom, Laura, felt the sting of those cold stares one Saturday morning.

Aisle after aisle, as they pushed their cart through a crowded grocery store, the two were met with gawking eyes . . . right along with some ill-timed, unflattering comments.

"Mommy, did you see that little girl?" blurted a child's voice.

"Shoosh," said an embarrassed mom.

"What's wrong with her face?"

"Lower your voice, please!"

"But why does she look that way?"

"I told you . . . *be quiet!*"

The fact is, Amy did stand out in a crowd. The little girl had Down syndrome, so her characteristic facial features—a flatter face and upward slanting eyes—were what most people noticed first. Yet to Laura, her baby girl was merely different, *not* defective. Amy came into the world with an extra chromosome, or as Laura often told others, "She has her very own 'something extra' that makes Amy unique."

Why can't others see what I see? Laura thought. *Why can't they see the precious, one-of-a-kind child sitting in this cart?*

As the two rolled up to the checkout, Laura and Amy were met with more stares. But this time, those gawking eyes were connected to a giant grin that stretched from cheek to cheek.

"Oh, isn't she an absolute beaut," a cashier said to Laura, stroking Amy's arm. The child beamed, her contagious smile practically lighting up the store. "She's melting my heart, Mom. I don't think I can let her go home with you!"

"Thank you," Laura replied. "She is my pride and joy, and she just turned six today. We're having a big birthday party to celebrate."

The cashier leaned closer to Laura and began to whisper: "Sorry about the other folks—their gawking and all. I saw them. I see everything from here."

"I'm getting used to it," Laura said, "which is kind of sad. I mean, how is my baby's Down's all that different from any other 'imperfection'? Just look around: everybody here is imperfect in one way or another."

The cashier looked up and practically stood at attention, almost as if a light bulb had clicked on inside. "You're absolutely right," she said. "Who gets to decide what's attractive and what isn't—or even what's 'normal'?"

"People are the ones who make up the definitions," Laura insisted. "And we're the ones who say it's bad to be below a certain height and better to be above it. We pretend there's this thing called 'normal,' yet it really doesn't exist. God, on the other hand, reminds us of how valuable we are. We are made in His image!"

Giving birth to Amy had driven home this truth for Laura. Yet the realization hadn't come easy. At first, learning that Amy had Down syndrome was almost too much for the young mother to bear.

It was a Saturday morning when Laura delivered what she believed to be the most beautiful baby on the planet. But then came the news that pulled the rug right out from underneath her.

As Laura's doctor stood by her bed, she could see from his expression that he had something difficult to share. "It's about Amy," he said. "The nurses have noticed some of the characteristics of Down syndrome."

Silence. Disbelieving silence.

"We can't be sure yet," he continued, "but there's a genetic test that will tell us with certainty."

Laura's mind was on autopilot as he spoke, but she managed to nod and even speak a few words: "Yes, please—let's do whatever it takes."

Desperate thoughts swirled through her brain: *Is this really happening? What quality of life will she have? How did we not see this?*

After the two longest weeks of her life, the test finally confirmed that Amy did, in fact, have Down's.

A new question swirled in Laura's brain: *What happens next?*

Her otherwise smooth-sailing life had just been interrupted, and she knew her world would never be the same.

But in the months and years that followed, Laura's heart changed.

She was well aware that Amy's extra copy of chromosome 21 wasn't what the world viewed as a blessing. Most saw it as a *dis*ability, literally a "want of ability."

Yet that label didn't apply to her little girl. Not only did Amy receive an extra set of genes; she also got an extra dose of courage, of gratitude, of service, of joy, of compassion.

And as far as Laura was concerned, where the eyes of the world saw a defect, the eyes of heaven saw perfection.[8]

Laura and her family emerged from this difficult season better and stronger.

Here's what Laura learned: being different just means that—we're different. "There's no need to add a value judgment on top of it," she says.

Laura believes that we are each a one-of-a-kind masterpiece, the very workmanship of God (Ephesians 2:10), knit together in our mother's womb, fearfully and wonderfully made (Psalm 139:13–14). We are valuable despite, or even because of, our differences.

My horses are precious reminders of what it means to have value in spite of imperfections. From a faraway perspective my horses look so picturesque, full of energy, their bodies dancing with light. But up close you will

WISDOM
FROM THE
HORSE FARM

The Holy Spirit reminds
us of our value to God.

see their scars and hear their old clicking bones. My white pony out there, he is not majestically rearing up with light glinting off his back. Nope, Spike is actually over thirty years old and missing an eye. In fact, almost all of the horses at my barn are there because they are no longer rideable due to age or injury. The horses have something that others would call a "defect." You would have lovingly suggested I get my head checked before laying down my hard-earned cash on any of them.

But the heart wants what the heart wants. I got *who* I wanted. These horses are safe for me to be around and are great companions, and although none of them are winning a beauty contest anytime soon, they are beautiful to me.

Their worth is not based on their abilities to jump, perform dressage, or race barrels, just as the value of any one of us is not based on our abilities either.

God wants what God wants, and He wanted you, so He made you. But God just doesn't end up with who He ends up with, and He doesn't "do what He can" with the mistakes that are created. When it comes to God, there are no mistakes.

God takes pieces of what the world calls broken and He paints for us this beautiful picture of what it means to be made in the image of God. Each one of us is valuable and purposeful; we are what God calls His masterpieces.

....

Lord, I praise You because of the wonderful way You created me. Help me to steer clear of the Enemy's lie that my differences make me defective. Help me to see the value in others. Amen.

22

TRADING FEAR FOR FAITH

Do not fear, for I am with you;
do not be dismayed, for I am your God.
I will strengthen you and help you;
I will uphold you with my righteous right hand.
ISAIAH 41:10

I love God, Tess thought to herself, *but I can't act and dress like a Christian clone.*

After two decades of being a Christ-follower, the young Nashville woman had grown weary of the strict rules and rigid regulations her church was teaching about clothing, behavior, and outward expression.

That's not what it means to be a good Christian, she thought. *The word* Christian *literally means "follower of Christ"—which is all about learning how to be Christlike.*

So, rather than being scared to death about what she should do or say, she left that church and started attending one that focused on what Christ Himself said was most important: "'You shall love the Lord your God with all your heart, and with all your soul, and with all your mind.' This is the greatest and first commandment. And a second is like it: 'You shall love your neighbor as yourself'" (Matthew 22:37–39 NRSV).

The change was liberating.

"Here's what I feel like," Tess told a friend over coffee one day. "Instead of just sitting in a service for an hour every Sunday with a preacher pounding the pulpit and waving a Bible—and that being the extent of my faith experience—I think it's more important that Christians *live out* Christ's teachings."

Tess's friend nodded in agreement. "Imagine the joy that comes from being Christlike," she said. "Imagine if Christians traded in fear for faith. All the lost, lonely people out there might actually be drawn to Jesus."

Joy. Love. Freedom. Suddenly, those words sounded so much better to Tess—so different from what she had been taught as a kid. Tess was taught that if she stayed in church, followed the rules, and didn't do the "don'ts," then she would experience holiness and the fullness of Christ.

In other words, her behavior and lifestyle would make her acceptable to God.

But a few years down the road, she sensed her first anxious pang: *Something just isn't adding up. Something is missing.*

She was well into her college years when the anxious pangs turned into nagging thoughts that she just couldn't dismiss: *I've been living the right way, but why can't I sense God's presence in my life anymore? Where did He go?*

Tess felt alone and separated from God, despite all her religious zeal.

In the days ahead she would pull out her journal and flip open her Bible, yet reading the Scriptures was a chore. At times God's Word felt lifeless, impractical, irrelevant. Her prayer life had lost its passion too. In fact, her whole faith had become rigid and mechanical.

> Tess felt alone and separated from God, despite all her religious zeal.

On one particular evening—a moment she'll never forget—an unthinkable fear flashed through her head: "Maybe I've lost Jesus."

There she sat, night after night—alone in her apartment, feeling as if she was completely cut off from her Lord and Savior, and convinced that He had left her.

She cried out to Him, yet God seemed silent. *What had happened?*

She had been searching for the "God of Rules"—a god whose love and favor were dependent on rules that He required—no, *demanded*—that she keep. In all honesty Tess was looking for a god who didn't really exist. She was searching in the dark.

As tears rolled down her cheeks, she cried out, "Show me how to love You! Show me how to soften my heart toward You. Show me how to know You . . . and hear You. Change me!"

As she wept the numbness slowly melted away.

In the weeks that followed, Tess began to understand the key that would guide her relationship with God: *She needed to fall in love with Jesus!*

Tess learned that she needed to pursue Christ as her closest companion and best friend in life. She must put all else aside to be with Him. He wanted to be the priority of her heart, even while she attended to the everyday business of life.

Have you fallen in love with Jesus? Tess learned what's gradually becoming more and more real in my own life: being in relationship with Jesus isn't about religion or following the rules. To be in *true relationship* with Jesus, we need to pursue *His heart, His passions, His character,* and *His truth.*

We need to be His hands, His feet, and a reflection of His love to others.

Just as He did for Tess, the Lord is gradually stripping away the masks, the false assumptions, the bad theology, the idols, and the chilly layers between Him and me, and little by little my heart is catching on fire for Him!

There's an amazing link between meditating on the Holy Scriptures and the intimate relationship with God that we seek—Bible reading, meditation, reflection, and prayer helps me engage in the *intimate conversation that flows through the sixty-six letters God has given us.*

Here's what author Ruth Hayley Barton suggests in her book *Sacred Rhythms*: It's important that Christ-followers long to hear a word from God that is personal and that takes them deeper into the connection that their souls crave. "The study of Scripture is important," Hayley points out, "but if we stop there, we will eventually hit a wall spiritually. . . . Our soul knows that there must be something more."[9]

Tess was ready for more. She was ready to walk in faith, not fear. And she was ready to share that liberating faith with a lost and broken world. I'm ready too.

Tess's story reminds me of how the Holy Spirit is moving me from religious rules to intimate relationship with God.

Several years ago I made the decision to board a newly purchased horse at a barn just north of town. I had space at my barn, but I was looking to train this horse for a specific purpose, and this place came recommended by a friend. In hindsight I should have heeded the warning in her body

WISDOM FROM THE HORSE FARM

The Holy Spirit moves us from religious rules to intimate relationship.

language when she suggested this trainer. In fact, her daughter actually winced. Her exact words were, "Well, maybe she has changed."

That response should have clued me in, but hindsight is always 20/20, as the saying goes, and also, a leopard doesn't change its spots.

Over the course of that first month of training, the trainer gave me the subtle impression that the horse was more than I could handle myself.

This barn trainer was one tough cookie. She let me know that since I didn't know enough about horses, I could get physically hurt. Lucky for me, she was the hero that wouldn't let that happen.

My kids were just toddlers at the time, and with Dan traveling a lot, it was a real sacrifice to make it over to her barn on dark winter nights to train, but I did it.

Six months into this journey, I began to have my doubts that this woman had my best interest at heart. Not only did I feel targeted financially, but I also felt this self-proclaimed horse whisperer was breaking me down mentally. During one training session she had me get off my horse so I could get on my hands and knees in the middle of her dirt arena. She wanted me down on all fours so I could "know what it's like to be a horse." It was humiliating.

I'd like to tell you that this was when I loaded up my horse and went home, but it wasn't.

Like Tess with her church board, I was still trying to score some points with this woman. Still trying to earn some form of respect as a real horse owner. I began to hate riding—hated horse people for sure—and I was losing any connection I had with my horse.

It's embarrassing to admit, but it took me another six months before I broke free.

I eventually had the epiphany that I was free to leave her barn at any time, so I took my horse and went home. I spent the next month just sitting in the pasture with him, resting in the peace and relief that come from liberation.

Anyone who has had that first life-altering encounter with Jesus knows what that feels like, to be free.

As followers of Jesus, sometimes we forget that we are free. We get lost in religion and build our worth through the "doing." I've done this myself and had to remind myself to go back to my first love, to go back to the cross. There is nothing we need to do to earn His forgiveness, because Jesus already provided it there.

Just reading my story next to Tess's, I see clearly why it's so easy to fall into religious traps. So many of us stop living like we're forgiven. If we are not in the Word daily, we can get so influenced by deceitful people. Instead of standing firm in what we know to be true, we allow outside parties to influence our malleable minds. We lose our focus and we put our hearts at risk of growing cold.

I know that's why I like witnessing to others so much. Each time I do, it's a reminder to me of what matters most in life.

You don't have to stay frozen in fear, and you don't need approval to be free. God says, "There is now no condemnation for those who are in Christ Jesus" (Romans 8:1).

If anyone tries to convince you otherwise, untie your horse and go home.

Lord, I want to pursue You as my closest companion and best friend in life. I want to put all else aside to be with You. I want You to be the priority of my heart. I know that being in relationship with You isn't about religion or following the rules. I need to be in true relationship with You—pursuing Your heart, Your passions, Your character, and Your truth. Amen.

PART 6

God's Spirit Makes Us Self-Controlled

23

ADDICTION AND GRACE

For the grace of God has appeared, bringing salvation
for all people, training us to renounce ungodliness and
worldly passions, and to live self-controlled, upright,
and godly lives in the present age, waiting for our blessed
hope, the appearing of the glory of our great God and
Savior Jesus Christ, who gave himself for us to redeem
us from all lawlessness and to purify for himself a people
for his own possession who are zealous for good works.
TITUS 2:11–14 ESV

Reno stepped through the doors of Notre Dame's Basilica of the Sacred Heart, looked up—and instantly froze in his tracks. *Toto, I have a feeling we're not in Indiana anymore,* he thought to himself.

Gothic arches rose high above his head, touching ornate paintings on the ceiling. A rainbow of colors shined through narrow stained glass all around him, illuminating frescoes of angels and scenes from the life of Christ. Reno felt as if he'd been swept away to a grand cathedral in Europe. Maybe even to heaven!

And to think, I'm still in the Hoosier State, he reminded himself.

The thirtysomething entertainer was in town to deliver his

high-energy comedy routine at a nearby night club. He couldn't help stopping by Notre Dame for a tour.

His eye caught an altar directly in front of him, and he knew what he had to do. *Pray,* he told himself. *It's been awhile since I've talked to God, and there's no better place to do it.*

Reno found a comfortable spot, knelt, and closed his eyes. As he ran down a long list of fears, hopes, and wants, something unexpected happened—an encounter he'd never, ever had in all his years of living as a Christian. Suddenly, an overwhelming feeling warmed his heart, and a distinct message rang in his ears. Reno sensed that God was right there next to him, speaking to him, nudging him. "Stop drinking!" God was telling him. "It's going to cause problems!"

Reno stood up—his body covered in goose bumps. He looked around the church in bewilderment. *Stop drinking? Wait. What?*

He quickly exited the church and walked along the Notre Dame campus, oblivious to all the people and the history and the beauty around him—his mind rattled and his heart pounding. *What should I do now?*

Reno pulled out his phone and punched the number of a close friend. "Dude, you're not going to believe what just happened . . ."

Yet by the end of the conversation, the two had laughed off the whole ordeal. "Honestly—a voice from God told you to stop doing the one thing you're really good at?" his buddy joked. "Not build an ark or part the Red Sea! But give up what makes you happy!"

As Reno slid his phone back into his pocket and climbed into his car, the smile on his face instantly disappeared and he caught his reflection in

> "Stop drinking!" God was telling him. "It's going to cause problems!"

the rearview mirror. His eyes were red, and his face looked pale and tired. *Happy?! I don't even know what that means!*

Yep, God had his attention. Reno knew the experience was real—and that it wasn't a laughing matter. *But never again touch a drop of alcohol? Is that even possible for me?*

That's when he retreated to what he'd always done when he felt as if his life was caving in on top of him: he crammed the memory deep down into a compartment somewhere in his heart. He'd find a place where he'd put things that didn't fit into what he wanted to do. And at the time, he believed he was in control.

Later, when he arrived at the venue, ready to perform, he had figured out a way to write off the experience at the church and justify his thoughts so he could do what he wanted—drink!

In the weeks and months that followed, the thought that God had spoken to him would pop its head up occasionally . . . until Reno would "whack-a-mole" it back down where he thought it belonged. He hid it deep inside—right along with all the guilt, fear, pride, pain, and arrogance that already stewed in there—until there were too many ingredients to hide. Then, over time they'd boil over—a nice, thick soup filled with anger, rage, and full-blown anxiety attacks. Magically, those feelings only went away when he got hammered!

Like so many other alcoholics, Reno fooled himself into thinking he was having the time of his life—carefree, laughing all the time, doing outrageous things that no sane person would ever imagine. Yet it was all a mask. He needed to cover up the fact that on one hand, he believed he was the greatest thing that ever happened to anybody. On the other hand, he was really just a scared, insecure little boy in a man's body.

His drinking continued for years, eventually growing from a want

WISDOM
FROM THE
HORSE FARM

The grace of God brings
salvation, healing, self-
control . . . and a whole
new direction as the
Lord guides our steps.

to a need. Reno got to the point where he couldn't do anything without a drink, and every occasion became an excuse to grab a drink and celebrate.

Then life smacked him directly in the face—and the message God had given him years earlier had become a reality: "Stop drinking! It's going to cause problems!"

Within a six-month period, everything exploded. At the time he was hosting a TV show that was supposed to be renewed. Suddenly, it was canceled. Then his circumstances went from bad to worse: his comedy tour ended, and his wife filed for divorce. An overwhelming feeling of "I've lost everything" began to take over. Reno knew the pain his kids would endure as his family broke apart.

Soon, his money dwindled, his drinking increased, and his mind swirled with catastrophic thoughts: *It's like the whole world is against me. I should just wake up and punch myself in the face before life gets a chance to. Why is this happening to me?*

Reno found himself drowning in self-pity. A broken ego, debt, and whiskey were getting the best of him. And to top it off, his doctor—who was watching Reno's liver fall apart—informed him that he had about five years to live.

Reno had wandered off the trail Jesus had set before him, and now he felt as if his foot was caught in a bear trap—making it impossible to backtrack. Yet deep in his gut, he knew Jesus hadn't abandoned him. Instead, he had left God.

Reno was brought up a Christian and always considered himself a believer—just on his terms. The seed of faith had been planted by his parents and grandparents when he was just a boy. Yet he had refused to let it grow. Reno had tried to quit drinking thousands of times on his own but had failed miserably each time. *How can I leave this misery and find faith?*

Once again, God had his attention—and even offered him a new way forward.

Those fresh steps began when Reno met a woman named Sandy. She had been widowed a couple of years earlier and was attending a church that Reno had visited. She didn't judge Reno for any of the things he had done. Not only that, over time Reno felt like he could be himself—not the pretend Reno he thought everyone wanted him to be. For the first time in his life, Reno felt as if he could be the "Deeper Me" he yearned to show the world. He finally wasn't afraid to reveal his insecurities and weaknesses.

Sandy prayed for him daily. And Reno began talking to God too.

He prayed as hard as he could for God to give him the strength to blindly enter a whole new world—without booze! And along the way he discovered that believers don't have to go to a cathedral or church for God to speak to them. He speaks to us every minute of every day—through our prayers, through the Bible, and through other people.

People like Sandy.

She eventually became Reno's wife, and she spent countless hours patiently encouraging him and explaining what it means to leave your fears, troubles, and problems at the altar. "Give it all to God," she'd tell him. "He'll take care of it."

So, Reno repeated the same prayer over and over: "Please, God, take this from me. I can't do it on my own."

Minutes of sobriety turned into hours, and eventually into days! Reno felt the way he had at Notre Dame: he sensed that God was right next to him, guiding his steps.

Reno was at the bottom looking up . . . with his hands reaching toward God. "You gotta take this." Slowly, as the fog in his mind cleared, God lifted him up.

> Along the way he discovered that believers don't have to go to a cathedral or church for God to speak to them.

What God did for Reno is profoundly amazing. Satan's ultimate goal is that we choose the path that leads to the glue factory. But while God doesn't promise us green pastures and clean boots here on earth, He does promise us paradise when we make the choice to stay safely in His corral.

....

Lord, thank You for bringing salvation for all people. Thank You for training us to renounce ungodliness and worldly passions and for showing us how to live self-controlled, upright, and godly lives. Thank You for blessed hope. Thank You for redeeming us from all lawlessness and for purifying us so we can do Your good works. Amen.

24

WHEN YOU'VE LOST YOUR WAY

*Those who live according to the flesh have their minds
set on what the flesh desires; but those who live in
accordance with the Spirit have their minds set on what
the Spirit desires. The mind governed by the flesh is
death, but the mind governed by the Spirit is life and
peace. The mind governed by the flesh is hostile to God;
it does not submit to God's law, nor can it do so.*

ROMANS 8:5–7

Gone. Everyone he loved and everything he had worked so hard to achieve in life had been ripped from him. The loss was almost too much to bear, yet Keith knew there was no one to blame but himself.

The forty-two-year-old Pennsylvanian curled up on a futon in his sister's basement (his temporary home) and read a passage of Scripture that popped up on his cell phone. It was 1 Peter 1:14–15: "So you must live as God's obedient children. Don't slip back into your old ways of living to satisfy your own desires. You didn't know any better then. But now you must be holy in everything you do, just as God who chose you is holy" (NLT).

The words stung. But that's usually what happens as medicine penetrates a wound. Keith took a deep breath and squeezed his eyes shut.

Everything was crystal clear now. It was so obvious how he had gotten to this miserable point, and he regretted every selfish step.

It all started when I chose to satisfy my own desires, not the will of God, he thought to himself. *I allowed myself to slip back into my old ways—just as Scripture warns us not to do. I let sinful choices take over.*

Eventually, those choices stole his family, his ministry, his money, his reputation.

It's one thing to make crazy decisions when we're young and naive and inclined to learn the hard way, he thought. *It's entirely different when we're middle-aged, supposedly "seasoned in the faith"—and in my case, a pastor.*

A secret struggle—pornography—had enslaved him. And even though Keith put up a desperate fight to break free, his world caved in on top of him. He brought shame on his kids and broke his wife's heart. The fact is, he had lied to everyone—over and over for so many years. That was hard to live with. He shuddered as he thought about the dark path he had veered onto, one that was leading him away from God.

Turning around and taking that first step back was the hardest thing he'd ever done.

A few weeks after his marriage ended, during one of Keith's darkest moments, his cell phone rang, and an unexpected name from his past appeared on his screen. The voice on the other end of the line was inviting him to come back home.

"Keith, it's Nikki—your sister."

At first he was speechless. The two hadn't talked in years.

"I want you to come home—come back to Pennsylvania. My life is different . . . better. And it's because of you. You helped me—eternally. And now it's my turn to help you."

Keith couldn't believe his ears. "You're taking me in?"

"Yep."

"But I've made such a mess of things," he told her. "I'm pretty screwed up right now."

"I get it," she responded. "I'm screwed up too. But I'm learning that God is pretty good at cleaning up our messes."

Today, Keith still sleeps on a futon in his sister's basement. It's a place where he has been able to heal, reflect on God's Word, and gradually find his way back.

"Spiritually, I spent years and years gutting through my struggles, trying to change," he told his sister during a long talk that lasted into the wee hours of the night. "But I attempted it in my own strength—not God's—and I failed every single time. I found myself constantly falling back into sin."

"I never knew any of this about you," his sister said. "To me, you were my older brother the pastor—the guy who had it all together."

"That's because I masked it all so well."

"No more masks, okay?"

"No more masks," Keith assured her. "And no more double life."

Keith knew things would never be the same. Emotional wounds and vivid memories constantly reminded him of all that he had lost. Old temptations kicked in whenever he was weak. Yet after years of feeling trapped by sin and utterly lost, Keith was finding his way back.

"From the world's perspective, there is no logical reason for me to follow Christ," he told his sister. "But I'm still fighting my guts out. I still want to know Christ and to follow Him."

One evening he realized the Bible verses he had been exploring recently had nailed his weaknesses. Verse after verse nudged him closer to Jesus, teaching him that Christ can redeem any sin. Deep in his heart of hearts, Keith knew that the Lord was restoring his broken life, and He was using Scripture, lots of prayer, and lots and lots of tears to do it.[10]

I'm reminded of another bittersweet story back on my farm. This one involves an old basset hound named Wilma.

Wilma liked to bury bones. She had a funny talent of always remembering where she buried them too. Wilma buried a bone in my mom's flower bed one summer. Two years later, when I pulled into the driveway, Wilma jumped out of the car and went to the spot where she buried that bone and with flowers flying began to reclaim her past.

I can see how people can look at a basset hound, nose full of dirt, and think that there's probably not much going on behind those droopy ears and eyes, but basset hounds are actually very intelligent and also very stubborn. Stubbornness has been bred into their DNA—which is why once a basset hound gets a whiff in its nose of something, like a juicy rabbit, it'll keep on following that scent to the end of the trail, for as long as it takes, no matter how dangerous.

Stubbornness is part of our DNA too. While Wilma buries bones, we bury sin. We hide it from others, or we dig it back up and beat ourselves over the head with things we've already been forgiven of.

WISDOM
FROM THE
HORSE FARM

When we lose our way,
the Lord nudges us back
on the right path.

Sin is a condition that exists when we reject God's goodness and His holy moral nature. It's part of our DNA, and if you don't think so, just imagine if you had a flashing sign on your forehead that advertised everything you thought. If that were the case, I'd be lucky to have two friends, and not even that many if their own thoughts called me out for my arrogance, my occasional stinky armpits, or the way I raise my kids.

When we repent we change our mind about Jesus Christ.

Jesus didn't come to make me happy. He didn't come down to earth to show me how to feed the poor. He came to save me!

In other words Jesus doesn't make me better than others; He makes me better than myself.

When we process the magnitude of that, we can't apologize to Him enough. That's when repentance changes our behavior. Jesus being punished for what I did makes me think twice before I make a sinful choice. But I'll admit that while that works most of the time, sinning is still a part of my DNA. I occasionally revert back to my old self and I have to start over. I call this failing forward.

I'm so glad that Keith was brave enough to share his story; I think it's a helpful reminder that we are all struggling. Keith was failing but is now moving forward in agreement with God.

If you are buried in sin, now is the time to focus on the One who took your place of punishment. Tell Him how sorry you are. That repentance will begin to change your behavior.

When it came to my old basset hound, after our visit, my mom would go out and dig up the bones Wilma buried. Next time we came by, Wilma would still go to the same spot where she'd buried her bones, but there would be nothing left for her to dig up, and my mom's flowers would stay intact.

Like Wilma, we remember where we bury the things we don't want to be seen. That's what Keith is working through right now. But once God takes those things away, there is nothing left for us to dig up.

Because of Christ's work on the cross, there is no need to dig up what has already been forgiven. After repentance, God doesn't have a bone to pick with Keith or anyone else who strives to live a life in agreement with God.

....

Lord, help me to live in accordance with the Spirit and to set my mind on what the Spirit desires. Thank You that, as Your Word says, I am not in the realm of the flesh but in the realm of the Spirit. If I ever find myself on the wrong path, nudge me back to You. Amen.

25

STRANDED . . . BUT NEVER ALONE

So I ask you to make full use of the gift that God gave you when I placed my hands on you. Use it well. God's Spirit doesn't make cowards out of us. The Spirit gives us power, love, and self-control.

2 TIMOTHY 1:6–7 CEV

Briana dangled helplessly from the driver's-side window of her crumpled pickup. She gasped for air and tried to scream, yet she struggled just to breathe.

Pain surged through every inch of her body—especially her left leg. *It feels stuck,* she thought, *like it's caught on something.*

The lean twenty-two-year-old blinked a couple of times and then squinted. Smoke and dust rose from the ground. Acrid smells of gasoline and burnt wires filled the air.

I'm outside, probably thrown from my truck. But why am I upside down? She turned her head and strained to look up: the mangled roof of what was once her Ford F-150 was sandwiched around her leg. *I'm trapped!*

She glanced frantically to her left and then to her right. *And I'm alone.*

On one side was the steep embankment her truck had rolled down. On the other, a plowed cornfield with long furrows of black dirt that stretch endlessly away from her.

Briana listened intently. Apart from the sound of her own labored breathing, *nothing*—no cars crunching down the gravel road, no barking dogs in the distance, not even the chirp of a lone cricket.

Suddenly, reality pressed in: *I'm stranded in the middle of nowhere on a country road nobody ever uses. I'm gonna die!*

She gasped for another breath—and coughed. She pushed against the truck with her hands and tried to pull herself up with her free leg, but her strength was gone.

"Somebody, anybody," she screamed, "I'm trapped. Help! Please, please . . ."

Briana threw off the covers and bolted up, her heart racing. She rubbed her eyes, then focused on a photo of her boyfriend on her nightstand. Sweat rolled down her neck.

I'm in bed, Briana consoled herself. *I'm at home . . . in my own room. It was just a—*

Briana trembled. If only it were a dream.

Why, God, why?

Will I have a normal life?

Will I get to do the things I love?

Will I ever walk again?

It frightened Briana to consider how everything could change in an instant. One second she was out for a drive on a sunny afternoon, laughing at what was on the radio and making plans for the future: *a fall wedding, one day a few children, dogs in the yard, a home of our own . . . maybe that little farmhouse I've always had my eye on . . . even horses in the pasture?*

And then, in an instant, the unthinkable happened. Before she knew it, she was facing challenges she never imagined enduring. Everyday activities she once took for granted—grabbing milk from the fridge, hugging a loved one, or even just *walking*—now take on much more meaning.

That's how it was for Briana. A freak accident just two miles from her Nebraska home changed her whole world. As she rumbled down a one-lane road that cut through rolling farmland, a speeding pickup appeared in her path. She twisted her steering wheel, narrowly missing the oncoming vehicle and launching her own truck into a ditch.

"Here's the hardest part," Briana told her boyfriend. "I never lost consciousness as it was happening. I remember every second—every detail of something I wish I could forget. And when my pickup stopped rolling, I heard the other truck drive away. At that point I knew I was in the middle of nowhere . . . stranded."

Injured, alone, and left for dead on the side of the road is more trauma than most people can handle. Yet Briana was both physically and emotionally strong. In fact, she worked as an EMT paramedic and was trained to keep her cool during stressful moments. It was the heartless act of two men fleeing the scene that really shook her up.

And to add insult to injury, Briana's challenges went from bad to worse in the days that followed. Once she was stabilized, doctors explained that her back had been broken and her spinal cord injured. She needed multiple surgeries, months of rehab . . . and faced the strong possibility of spending the rest of her days in a wheelchair.

She was young and in the prime of her life. She had no clue that

WISDOM FROM THE HORSE FARM

The Holy Spirit turns fear into peace, chaos into self-control.

anything like that could happen to her. Briana had tested for the fire department the week before—so the thought of never walking again was more than she could handle.[11]

It seems as if struggle and fear go hand in hand. Fear is one of Satan's favorite tools to use against us. But the good news is, God tells us—from the beginning of the Bible to the end—that He has conquered fear and has overcome the trials and tribulations of this world. He promises He'll never abandon us in our time of need.

When Briana realized the other truck was gone, she knew she was in trouble. She struggled to breathe and was pretty certain that at least her leg was broken. She attempted several times to pull herself up and break free but couldn't. She needed help, quickly. "I just sort of let go and hung there—probably for ten minutes," she says. "And that's when God intervened."

Another driver who'd also taken a wrong turn that day—a man looking for his sister's house—happened to see her. Briana knew she would be okay.

Eight months after being admitted to a rehabilitation center, Briana took her first step.

Gradually, she learned to bend her knees and lift her feet. She began with very small steps and worked herself up to more difficult challenges. At first, it seemed kind of silly to her: walk from the bed to the door of the hospital room and then back to her bed. Then, it was to the door and back twice. Each success was a big accomplishment, especially considering that doctors feared she might never walk again.

And six months later—a year and a half after her accident—Briana walked down the aisle. "I married the love of my life," she says. "He never left my side, coaching me with each step . . . and holding me when the panic would strike."

Briana says medicine, prayer, and the support of those she loves made all the difference in the world. "I'm on a healing path," she says, "and that's a good place to be."

Briana is an inspiration to me. She has encouraged me to keep pressing forward in spite of life's challenges.

In fact, I have to pep-talk myself occasionally by saying, "Saddle up anyways." It's a shortened version of my favorite John Wayne saying: "Courage is being scared to death but saddling up anyways."

Easy to say, but any new trouble that comes along actually requires a true sense of peace in order to put your feet into those life stirrups and say, "Giddyup!"

Years ago, when I was in the thick of some significant digestive issues, I struggled with a deep fear of being abandoned. I had all these questions and doubts swirling through my head and an Enemy that was more than happy to fan the flames. I didn't want to be a burden to my family. The questions and worries that repeatedly flogged my very soul were, "How could I possibly be attractive to my husband right now? He's going to leave me; he didn't sign up for this. Will I have the energy required to be a good mother? My kids are going to resent me . . ."

As a follower of Jesus, there are times when those types of lies roll through my head. I make it a point to ask myself, *Who told you that?* None of the lies above reflect the character of God.

I'm not exactly sure how deep horses think or how they process their circumstances, but I have looked deep into the eyes of a horse who had a significant leg injury. I wondered how much of that fear in his eyes was the fear of being isolated from the herd or maybe his fear of being abandoned. I can relate.

Injured horses never seem to have peace or the ability to relax. Their weakness instinctually lets them know that because they are injured, they are now prime mountain lion food. Their fear makes them isolate themselves without even knowing what they are doing, and eventually they will meet their demise.

That gives me a visual of how we are spiritually stalked by the enemy. When that nasty pile of dung, the devil, spots an insecurity or an injury to our spiritual armor, here comes the prowling lion, ready to steal our peace.

Just like Briana, in our weakness, we start to isolate ourselves without realizing what that sneaky snake is up to, and we see how fast he moves in.

But Jesus tells us that if we believe in who He is and what He's done, we can have perfect peace through hard times. Unlike that self-isolating horse, we are never alone.

Lord, I take comfort in Your Word, especially this encouraging reminder from John 14:27: "Peace I leave with you; my peace I give to you. Not as the world gives do I give to you. Let not your hearts be troubled, neither let them be afraid" (ESV). Fill my heart with peace when my life spins out of control. Remind me that even though I may be temporarily stranded, with You I am never alone. Amen.

NOTES

1. "Benefits of Equine Therapy: 5 Lessons Only a Horse Teaches," Promises Behavioral Health, November 25, 2020, https://www.promisesbehavioralhealth.com/addiction-recovery-blog/lessons-equine-therapy/.

2. Max Lucado, *Fearless: Imagine Your Life Without Fear* (Nashville: Thomas Nelson, 2009), 10.

3. Adapted from Arnie Cole and Michael Ross, *Unstuck: Your Life, God's Design, Real Change* (Bloomington, MN: Bethany House, 2012), 170–73.

4. "Kelly" and "Jeff" are pseudonyms. Their names were changed to protect their identities.

5. Lynn Baber, *Amazing Grays, Amazing Grace: Lessons in Leadership, Relationships, and the Power of Faith Inspired by the Love of God* (Lynn Baber, 2017), 79-80.

6. Adapted from Julie Brown Patton, "Paralyzed Rodeo Champion Is Back in Saddle: 'My Faith in God Has Grown,'" March 10, 2016, *The Gospel Herald*, https://www.gospelherald.com/articles/62816/20160310/paralyzed-rodeo-champion-is-back-in-saddle-my-faith-in-god-has-grown.htm.

7. Adapted from Michael Ross, *Faith That Breathes* (Uhrichsville, OH: Barbour, 2004), 45–46.

8. "Laura" and "Amy" are pseudonyms. Their names were changed to protect their identities.

9. Ruth Haley Barton, *Sacred Rhythms: Arranging Our Lives for Spiritual Transformation* (Downers Grove, IL: InterVarsity Press, 2006), 49.

10. "Keith" is a pseudonym. His name was changed to protect his identity.

11. Adapted from Arnie Cole and Michael Ross, *Worry-Free Living: Find Relief from Anxiety and Stress for You and Your Family* (Franklin, TN: Authentic, 2014), 77–79.